THE WAR ON
TERRORISM

ISSUES FOR THE 90s

THE WAR ON TERRORISM

Michael Kronenwetter

JULIAN MESSNER

JULIAN MESSNER and colophon are trademarks of
Simon & Schuster, Inc. Design by Claire Counihan
Manufactured in the United States of America.

Lib. ed. 10 9 8 7 6 5 4 3 2

Library of Congress Cataloging-in-Publication Data

Kronenwetter, Michael.
The war on terrorism/Michael Kronenwetter.
p.   cm. — (Issues for the 90s)
Bibliography: p. 122
Includes index.
Summary: Discusses how terrorism has become more common, more dangerous, and
more international over the past few decades. Examines U.S. policy and responses
towards terrorist acts, profiles specific terrorist groups, and offers strategies for
combatting the violence.
1. Terrorism—History—20th century—Juvenile literature.
2. Terrorism—Prevention—History—20th century—Juvenile
literature.   3. World politics—1945– —Juvenile literature.
4. Word politics—1975–1985—Juvenile literature.   [1. Terrorism.
2. World politics—1945– 3. World politics—1975–1985.]   I. Title.
II. Series.
HV6431.K7   1989
909.82—dc20   89-9470
                                                                 CIP
ISBN 0-671-69050-7 (lib. bdg.)   AC

CONTENTS

THE WAR ON
TERRORISM

CHAPTER ONE

NATIONS

UNDER ATTACK

A NEW AGE OF TERRORISM

THE weapons of the terrorist—violence, brutality, and fear—are as old as human society. The ancient history of Asia, the Middle East, and Europe is filled with acts that would today be considered terrorism. But both the nature and extent of terrorism have changed during the past few decades. Terrorism has become more common and much more dangerous than it used to be. It also has become increasingly international.

The new age of terrorism dawned at 4:30 in the morning of September 5, 1972. It was then that a group of silent men climbed over a fence surrounding Munich's Olympic Village, where athletes from all over the world were sleeping.

The seventeenth modern Olympic Games were being held in Munich that year. Like all Olympic Games, they were regarded as more than just a major athletic event. They were a symbol of international friendship and peaceful competition.

The choice of West Germany as the site for that year's games was symbolic. Germany had led the world into the two bloodiest wars in human history and had been almost destroyed in the process. West Germany had been peacefully rebuilt out of the ashes of World War II, a war it had started. Having the Olympics in West Germany was a powerful symbol of the triumph of international peace and cooperation over the evil of war.

Munich also was a powerful symbol for the men who climbed over the Olympic Village fence that morning. So was the choice of their soon-to-be victims. The fence climbers could have been athletes themselves. They even carried athletic bags. But they were not athletes, and their innocent-looking bags did not contain athletic equipment. They were terrorists, and their bags contained automatic weapons and hand grenades.

It was just about 5 o'clock in the morning when they knocked on the door of one of the rooms in which the Israeli Olympic team was staying. The knock was answered by the team's wrestling coach. Even half asleep as he was, he quickly realized what was happening, and he yelled to his fellow Israelis to escape. Incredibly, some did. Instantly awake, they lurched out other doors or scrambled through open windows. But eleven of the others were not so quick to awaken, so fast to move, or so lucky. Two of them, including the coach who had shouted out the warning that saved the others, were shot and killed on the spot. Nine others were taken captive.

The Munich authorities heard of the horrible events at the Olympic Village within moments. Within moments after that, the rest of the world heard as well. News of the murders and kidnappings was speeded by the fact that thousands of newspeople from all over the world were gathered in Munich for the Olympics. Among them was a large crew from the American ABC television network. They were there to broadcast the sporting events live, not just to the United States but to scores of other countries as well. They ended up broadcasting a nightmare.

Images of hooded terrorists sent a chilling message around the world when members of the Black September organization attacked Israeli athletes at the Munich Olympics in 1972. AP/Wide World Photos

By midmorning, the terrorists, now wearing ski masks to conceal their faces from the television cameras, had declared their cause. They were Palestinians, they said, members of an organization called Black September. They wanted the Jewish state of Israel disbanded and its territory, which they claimed as their own homeland, returned to the Palestinian people. More immediately, they demanded that some 200 of their fellow Arabs be released from Israeli prisons, with safe passage for themselves and their hostages to get out of Germany. If these demands were not granted soon, they said, they would begin killing their hostages.

By evening the German government had worked out an agreement with the terrorists. Tens of millions of people around the world watched their television sets in horrified fascination as the terrorists and their captives were loaded onto two German helicopters and flown to a NATO air base near Munich. There, the terrorists were told, they would be allowed to board an airplane to fly to Cairo, Egypt.

Secretly, however, the German government had stationed sharpshooters at the air base with orders to kill the terrorists. But when the sharpshooters opened fire, they only managed to hit three of the eight terrorists. The rest remained hidden in the two helicopters, along with all nine of the hostages.

In the eerie gun battle that followed on the darkened runway, one of the helicopters and all the hostages aboard it were destroyed by a terrorist hand grenade. The other was riddled with gunfire. All nine hostages, five of the terrorists, and one German policeman were killed.

A LESSON LEARNED

The assult on the Israeli athletes was not the first modern terrorist attack. There had been hijackings of airliners in the Middle East and elsewhere for years. It wasn't even the bloodiest modern terrorist attack. Four months before Munich, in May 1972, Japanese terrorists from the Army of the Red Star had attacked in Lod Airport in Tel Aviv, Israel, with guns and hand grenades. Twenty-five people, most of them Puerto Rican tourists, were killed, and more than seventy others were wounded. Two years before that, forty-seven people had died when a terrorist bomb blew up a Swiss jetliner.

From the point of view of the terrorists themselves, however, the Munich attack was the most successful terrorist action of modern times. It didn't really matter to them that their demands had not been met, that the 200 prisoners had not been released, and that the terrorists did not even get safely out of Germany. The real reason the terrorists had struck at the Olympics was to draw attention to the Palestinian cause, a goal they achieved beyond their wildest dreams.

The nightmare in Munich was shared by at least 500 million

people watching on television around the globe. Before Munich, most of them probably had never heard of the Palestinian cause. After Munich, most would never forget it.

The events at Munich proved that a single terrorist action, cleverly planned and daringly executed by a small band of people, could accomplish as much as the movement of a large army. That is why the Munich attack was the dawn of a new age of terrorism. It was a lesson that terrorists everywhere were quick to learn.

A DIFFERENT KIND OF WAR

Many people saw the attack at Munich as a battle in a war. It is a different kind of war—against a different kind of enemy—from the wars that nations of the world are used to fighting.

It is a war in which no armies meet on any battlefield. No tanks move across any borders. No planes swoop low to drop their deadly cargoes on helpless cities. No missiles streak across the skies.

Instead, there are isolated bursts of sudden violence. A bomb is exploded in an office building or a downtown shopping mall. An innocent civilian is gunned down while walking across a street in some foreign capital. A band of gunmen open fire with submachine guns in a crowded restaurant. A jetliner is hijacked or blown up with all its passengers aboard.

This war is not fought by soldiers, but by individuals or small groups of people called terrorists. They claim to represent mysterious organizations, with strange, often romantic-sounding names: names like the Tupamaros or the Symbionese Liberation Army or Black September. They strike quickly, usually without any warning, and always without mercy. Then they disappear until they are ready to strike again.

Their attacks often are not directed against military targets but against civilians. Americans are among the most common targets of terrorist attacks. Many of those attacks against

Americans take place abroad. Some occur in the Middle East, some in Central or South America, and some in Europe. Altogether, in recent decades American citizens or property has been attacked in at least seventy-two different countries around the world.

Terrorist attacks are not limited to American targets or to the citizens of any one country. The attack in Munich, after all, was directed against Israel and took place on West German soil. At times, it seems, the real target of the terrorists' war is western civilization itself. This was suggested by former President Ronald Reagan when he declared, "We consider these murders, hijackings, and abductions an attack on all western civilizations by uncivilized barbarians."

Even that evaluation, however, is too simple. Western countries are not the only targets of terrorist attacks. Terrorists have attacked in Asia, the Middle East, Africa, and even the countries of the communist eastern bloc. At times, it seems, the terrorists consider everyone their enemy. The terrorist war is not only a war without borders, at times it seems to be a war without purpose as well.

But is it really? This book will explore that question, and these others. What is terrorism? Who are the terrorists? What do they want? Why do they do the things they do? Most important, what can be done to stop them?

WHAT IS TERRORISM?

Terrorism can be a difficult word to define. The governments of the world have never come up with a definition on which they can all agree. As one former American diplomat has said, "It may be hard to define, but it's not hard to recognize it when you see it."

A very broad definition of terrorism is this: It is the planned use of violence to frighten and intimidate others in order to achieve political ends.

It is as important to understand what terrorism is *not* as to understand what it *is*. Terrorism is not the isolated act of an individual, acting alone out of personal motives. It is not a large-scale political demonstration or riot, however destructive that may be. It is not an atrocity committed in anger by a regular military force in the course of fighting a war. These actions share some characteristics with terrorism, but none of them is terrorism itself.

Four major characteristics of the kinds of terrorism will be discussed in this book:

1. Terrorism is essentially political. That is, it is designed to influence public opinion, the actions of governments, or both. It is a form of propaganda—even a kind of psychological warfare. It often achieves its purpose by unsettling society and inspiring terror among the population. The French-Algerian terrorists known as the Delta Commandos, for example, exploded "plastique" bombs in Arab neighborhoods of Algeria in the 1950s. These attacks were designed to frighten the Arabs from attempting to win independence from Algeria's French colonial government. At the same time, the Arab terrorists of the *Front Liberation National* (FLN) set off the explosive, plastique, in French neighborhoods to frighten the French into leaving.

2. Terrorism is a clandestine activity. Terrorists surround themselves with secrecy. Their crimes are public, but their identities and numbers are hidden. That is why the Black September terrorists in Munich wore hoods and why they gave no details about other members of their groups. Even when governments commit terrorism, as they sometimes do, it is done unofficially. It is not openly acknowledged as a governmental act, even when everyone knows that a government is behind it. The Libyan government, for example, sends out assassins to murder enemies of Libyan leader Muammar Qadaffi living abroad. These acts are

meant to threaten Qadaffi's other enemies, so the government does not try to disguise the killings. At the same time, the Libyan government does not admit to carrying them out.

3. Terrorism almost always involves violence of a particularly brutal and merciless kind. Terrorism is meant to torture the imagination of everyone who hears about it. That is why the Mau Mau terrorists of Kenya sometimes slaughtered whole families of English colonists, including infant children, in their efforts to drive the colonists out in the 1950s.

4. Terrorism tends to involve violence against civilians or other noncombatants. People expect military forces to face danger. If terrorists hope to terrorize the general public, their actions must reach beyond the military into the civilian population itself. They must give *everyone* the sense that *anyone* can become a victim of terrorism at any time. That was one reason the Army of the Red Star attacked the innocent foreign passengers at Lod Airport.

WHAT IS A TERRORIST?

Terrorists are people who commit terrorist acts. That may sound obvious, but it is not. Many people don't define those involved in violence as terrorists according to what they *do* but according to why they do it. Those people who are opposed to a group's politics—the cause the group is fighting for—are quick to condemn the group as terrorist whenever it engages in any form of violence. Those people who approve of the group's cause are often reluctant to classify that group as terrorist, no matter what it does.

When the German Nazis occupied France during World War II, French resistance fighters assassinated French citizens who were friendly to the Germans. The Germans looked upon these French fighters as terrorists.

In recent times, the Sandinista government of Nicaragua called the U.S.-backed Contras "terrorists" for their attacks against the government and its supporters. The Reagan administration, however, consistently defended the Contras as "freedom fighters."

In this book, we will try to avoid that kind of political judgment. Here, people and groups will be classified as terrorists if their actions fit the definitions given above, no matter how good, or how bad, their particular cause may be.

Some of the terrorist groups we will talk about in this book are not *just* terrorists. Many of them have worthwhile political or social goals and engage in legitimate activities as well. For our purposes, however, if they carry out terrorist activities, they will be considered as terrorists.

THE HISTORY OF TERRORISM IN AMERICA

The new age of terrorism caught many Americans by surprise. Americans had been accustomed to thinking of terrorism as a foreign thing. It was something that happened in Europe or the Middle East, not in the United States. In fact, the history of the United States is as studded with terrorist activity as the history of most other places.

The Indians on the western frontier practiced a form of terrorism, attacking unescorted wagon trains and isolated homesteads in efforts to frighten off settlers. Even scalping, a European practice that was adopted by some Indian tribes, had the terrorist purpose of inspiring fear in the enemy.

In the mid-nineteenth century, both pro-slavery and anti-slavery forces used terrorist tactics in the battle over whether

Kansas would enter the Union as a slave state or as a free state. The violence was so widespread that it earned the territory the pathetic nickname, "Bleeding Kansas."

John Brown and his sons were the most famous of the anti-slavery terrorists. Like many other terrorists, before and since, Brown thought of himself as an agent of God. His belief that God had sent him to destroy slavery made him feel justified in whatever tactics he might use. Those tactics included the cold-blooded murder of five pro-slavery men in what became known as the "Pottawatomie Massacre." The killings were clearly terrorist acts. Brown declared that they had been committed specifically to "cause a restraining fear" in the pro-slavery forces.

Following the Civil War, the Ku Klux Klan, the Kights of the White Camelia, and other white "night riders" launched campaigns of terror against the freed slaves in the South. They were determined to ensure white dominance by frightening black people out of asserting their new legal rights. The lynchings, cross burnings, and arsons that began in the 1860s remained commonplace in many areas of the South for nearly a century.

The efforts of industrial workers to organize into labor unions in the late 1800s and early 1900s were often met by terrorist tactics on the part of their employers. Companies like Carnegie Steel and the big coal mining companies of the Appalachian Mountains hired "goons" to beat up and even murder labor organizers.

Some unions were accused of using terrorist tactics in return. The printing plant of the *Los Angeles Times* newspaper was dynamited, for example, by workers who were angry with its anti-union stand. Many of the accusations of terrorism were directed at the so-called Wobblies of the Industrial Workers of the World. Although much of that criticism was unjustified, other labor groups, like the secret organization of coal miners known as the Molly Maguires, clearly used terror as a way of fighting for their rights.

Probably the most famous incident of labor-connected violence took place in Chicago on May 1, 1886. On that day, a meeting of workers was held in Haymarket Square to protest the killing of four striking workers by police the day before. When a large group of policemen tried to break up the meeting, someone threw a bomb. Seven of the policemen were killed. Scores more were injured. Enraged and frightened, several policemen fired into the crowd of workers, killing four of them.

In 1950, two Puerto Rican terrorists, devoted to making Puerto Rico an independent country, attempted to assassinate President Harry Truman. In 1954, four others fired guns onto the floor of the U.S. House of Representatives, wounding five Congressmen. In the years since, the small Puerto Rican nationalist group, called the FALN after the initials of its name in Spanish, Fuerzas Armadas de Liberación Nacional, has claimed responsibility for scores of bombings and several deaths, mostly in New York City.

In the late 1960s, anger at racism, economic inequality, and the American involvement in the Vietnam War prompted many young Americans to join radical organizations. A few of these groups, such as the one known as the Weathermen (or Weather Underground), used terrorism, including bombings, to make their political points.

For the most part, the American terrorism of the 1960s was directed more against property than against people. The targets were often symbolic: buildings that belonged to the government or to the big businesses the radicals believed were profiting from social injustice and the war. The attacks were violent, and a number of people were injured and even killed.

On a single day in November 1969, bombs went off in the RCA building, the General Motors building, and the Chase Manhattan Bank building, all in New York City.

In the middle of the night of August 24, 1970, a bomb exploded in the mathematics building of the University of Wisconsin in Madison. It killed a student who was working late. The building had been chosen for attack because the university's mathematics department did research for the U.S. Army.

In May 1972, a bomb went off in the Pentagon building in Washington, D.C.

These and scores of other bombings and attacks made many Americans aware of terrorism for the first time. Most still thought of them as the violent acts of a few young crackpots, rather than any serious threat to the peace and security of the United States. The events at Munich changed that attitude. By the mid-1970s, many Americans had come to believe that the United States was in the front lines of the war on terrorism.

TERRORISM SINCE 1972

The years since the massacre in Munich have seen a dramatic increase in terrorist activities around the world. According to the U.S. Central Intelligence Agency (CIA), there was a total of sixty-four international kidnappings in the five years before Munich. In the five years after 1972, there were 152.

Many of the new terrorist acts were committed in the United States. A study by an Army terrorism expert, Colonel James B. Motley, showed that terrorist-related crimes in the United States increased threefold from 1973 to 1976.

The increase in terrorist bombings may have been even more dramatic. The mid-1970s were the years of the bomb in the United States. Terrorists claimed responsibility for at least eighty-nine bombings in 1975 alone. That was about four times the number in 1973. Among them was a bombing that killed eleven people and wounded more than four times that many in New York's La Guardia Airport in December 1975.

Not all the terrorist attacks in the United States were directed against Americans. Some were aimed at foreign political figures and diplomats. On September 21, 1976, Orlando Letelier, a Chilean opponent of his country's right-wing government, was blown up by a car bomb in Washington, D.C. In January 1982, a Turkish consul general was murdered in his car in Los Angeles. In May of the same year, a Turkish honorary general consul was shot to death in a car in Boston. Both killings were claimed by the Justice Commandos of the Armenian Genocide, a terrorist group bent on avenging a slaughter of between 800,000 and 1,500,000 Armenians by the Ottoman Turks in 1915.

While foreigners were coming under attack in the United States, American officials were coming under attack abroad. Both the American Embassy and the U.S. ambassador's home in Lima, Peru, were damaged by bombs in August 1981. Three months later, shots were fired at the charge d'affaires of the American Embassy in Paris, France. Then in January 1982, an assistant military attaché at the same embassy was gunned down in the street.

The U.S. Department of State recorded over 5,000 incidents of terrorism around the world in the decade from 1975 to early 1985. That number was probably an underestimation. In 1984, for example, another report claimed that terror-dealing death squads had killed as many as 4,000 people in Indonesia alone.

The number of terrorist incidents kept climbing throughout the early 1980s. A 1985 study by the Rand Corporation showed international terrorism growing at the frightening rate of 12 percent to 15 percent a year since Munich—the rate was accelerating rapidly. The State Department recorded some 600 incidents of international terrorism in 1984 and 800 in 1985. They included one of the most deadly terrorist acts in history: a bomb placed on an Air India jet from Toronto, Canada, to Bombay, India, that killed 329 people. If September 1972 was the dawn of the new age of terrorism, the mid-1980s seemed to be its high noon.

The terror has hardly lessened since 1985. In places like Beirut, Lebanon, the casualties have mounted so fast that many are not even reported in most of the world's press. The following are just a few of the thousands of terrorist incidents that *have* been reported in the past few years:

- February and March 1986—Several bombs went off in crowded areas of Paris. At least two people were killed and forty-nine were wounded. Another bomb was discovered at the Eiffel Tower but was disarmed before it could explode.

- April 1986—A bomb was placed on a Trans-World Airlines flight from Rome to Athens by a group calling itself the Arab Revolutionary Cells. The bomb exploded over Greece, blowing a hole in the side of the plane. Four people, including a nine-month-old baby, were sucked out of the hole and killed.

- September 1986—Two terrorists murdered twenty-one worshipers in a synagogue in Istanbul, Turkey, and then blew themselves up.

- August 1987—A band of left-wing Naxalite terrorists killed ten policemen in Andhra Pradesh, India. In early 1988, the Indian government reported that the Naxalites had killed more than 200 people in recent years.

- December 1987—Right-wing terrorists belonging to the Mozambican National Resistance first mined and then raided a railroad train in the African nation of Mozambique. Twenty-two passengers were killed, and more than seventy others were injured.

- March 1988—British agents gunned down two unarmed members of the Irish Republican Army (IRA) in Gibraltar. This essentially terrorist act was committed, the British government announced, to stop the IRA men from carrying out a terrorist murder of their own.

Later the same year—on December 21, 1988—terrorists planted a bomb on PanAm's Flight 103 out of Frankfurt, West Germany. It blew up over the village of Lockerbie, Scotland, killing 270 people. Many of the victims were villagers, who were killed on the ground.

Policemen in Lockerbie, Scotland, guard the wreckage of Pan Am's flight 103 from Frankfurt to New York after a terrorist bomb exploded causing the crash in December 1988. AP/Wide World Photos

AMERICAN REACTION—A STUDY IN CONFUSION

The world had known terrorism before the Munich Massacre, but never terrorism like the terrorism that followed. Never had it come from so many different directions. Never had it affected so many different countries. Governments around the world were thrown into confusion.

Different nations tried different ways to deal with the growing menace. Some tried negotiating with the terrorists. Some tried refusing to negotiate with them. Some tried police methods. Some tried military crackdowns. Some even tried giving the terrorists what they wanted. Nothing that any of them did seemed to work for long.

In the United States, three different presidential administrations tried and failed to halt the threat to Americans from the rising tide of terrorism around the world. Their failures were often dramatic.

It was partly the fear of home-grown American terrorists that led Richard Nixon's administration into many of the excesses that were revealed in the Watergate scandal. In the late 1960s and early 1970s, the government spied on American opponents of the Nixon administration and carried out many illegal activities against them. The discovery of these practices eventually forced President Nixon to resign from office before he could be impeached.

Jimmy Carter's administration tried to take a more practical, police officer-like approach to terrorists. After scores of Americans were taken hostage in the U.S. Embassy in Teheran, Iran, the public began to see his policies as weak. Carter refused to ransom the hostages but was unable to find any other way to get the hostages released. The government of Iran supported the hostage takers, and Carter was unable to find a way to force Iran to get the hostages released.

Eventually, a military attempt to rescue the hostages failed. Many Americans were outraged. They couldn't understand how a relatively small country in the Middle East could defy the most powerful nation on earth by holding Americans prisoner for more than a year. Many political observers believe that it was Carter's failure to get the hostages home that cost him his chance for reelection.

VICE PRESIDENT'S TASK FORCE ON COMBATING TERRORISM

Following Carter the next president, Ronald Reagan, was elected on the promise that he would be tougher with terrorists. As president, he proclaimed a strict, uncompromising policy. He would never deal with terrorists, he proclaimed, and he warned that any terrorists who attacked Americans would do so at their own peril.

It seemed to many observers that the U.S. government was ready to treat the battle against terrorism the way many of the terrorists did: as a war. If the terrorists of the world were going to wage war on the United States, that country would wage its own war in return.

Nevertheless, terrorist attacks against Americans continued—and even worsened—during Reagan's first several years in office. In July 1985, the president set up a Cabinet-level commission, known as the Vice President's Task Force on Combating Terrorism. Chaired by then Vice President George Bush, it included among its members the U.S. secretaries of state, defense, treasury, and transportation; the director of the Central Intelligence Agency; and the chairman of the Joint Chiefs of Staff, along with many other high government officials and advisers.

The task force issued a public report in February 1986. While making some organizational and other recommendations for improving the American response to terrorism, the report concluded that the "national program" already in place was "well conceived and working." It insisted that "the U.S. policy and program to combat terrorism is tough and resolute."

The report went on to describe that policy, in what amounts to the declared position of the U.S. government in regard to terrorism:

> The U.S. position on terrorism is unequivocal: firm opposition to terrorism in all its forms and wherever it takes place. Several National Security Decision Directives as well as statements by the President and senior officials confirm this policy:
> The U.S. Government is opposed to domestic and international terrorism and is prepared to act in concert with other nations or unilaterally [alone]...to prevent or respond to terrorist acts.
> The U.S. Government considers the practice of terrorism by any person or group a potential threat to its national security, and

will resist the use of terrorism by all legal means available.

States that practice terrorism or actively support it will not do so without consequence. If there is evidence that a state is mounting or intends to conduct an act of terrorism against this country, the United States will take measures to protect its citizens, property and interests.

The U.S. Government will make no concessions to terrorists. It will not pay ransoms, release prisoners, change its policies or agree to other acts that might encourage additional terrorism . At the same time, the United States will use every available resource to gain the safe return of American citizens who are held hostage by terrorists.

The United States will act in a strong manner against terrorists without surrendering the basic freedoms or endangering democratic principles and encourages other governments to take similar stands.

U.S. policy is based upon the conviction that to give in to terrorists' demands places even more Americans at risk. This no-concessions policy is the best way of ensuring the safety of the greatest number of people.

Even while declaring that "unequivocal" policy, however, the Reagan administration was violating it.

DEALING WITH TERRORISTS

Within two years of his election, President Reagan had a hostage crisis of his own to deal with. In June 1982, David Dodge, the president of the American University of Beirut, Lebanon, was kidnapped by terrorists there. (See Chapter Three for a detailed explanation of the complicated terrorist situation in Lebanon.)

A year later, Dodge was freed. He was only the first in a long line of Americans and other foreigners who would be kidnapped in that troubled country. Like him, some of them were released within a year or two, but many of them were not. By the start of 1986, at least five Americans were being held prisoner in Lebanon. Another American prisoner, a CIA employee named

William Buckley, had apparently already been tortured to death.

Publicly, the U.S. government strongly condemned the kidnappings and held firm to its declared policy that it would make no deals with terrorists or with any government that actively supported them. Behind the scenes, however, it was behaving very differently. It was not only making deals with the government of Iran, which was supporting the terrorists, but it was supplying Iran with military equipment.

In the summer of 1985, even before he established the Vice President's Task Force on Combating Terrorism, President Reagan authorized the shipment of Hawk missiles to Iran. Hawks are anti-aircraft weapons, used for defense against low-flying airplanes. In return, the Iranian government was to use its "influence" with the kidnappers in Lebanon to get the American hostages there released.

This deal, of course, was made in great secrecy. It was so secret that even Noel Koch, the Pentagon's top man in the fight against terrorism, was surprised when he heard about it. Iran's government, after all, was one of the world's leading sponsors of terrorism. American officials had even been urging all its allies to refuse to provide Iran with arms, but it was secretly providing arms itself.

Even more shocking was the fact that the U.S. government was supplying arms as part of a deal for hostages: the kind of deal it was publicly promising that it wouldn ever make.

The deal was finally made public late in 1986, when a report of it was published in a small journal in Beirut. At first, the Reagan administration denied the reports, but finally had to admit that they were true. Even then, President Reagan insisted that he had not actually traded arms for hostages. What he meant was unclear, since he also claimed that he had been led to make the deal by his deep concern for the safety of the hostages. In any case, the embarrassed president announced that no more arms would be sent to Iran under any circumstances.

The revelation that the "get tough" president had made *any* arms deal with Iran resulted in a major scandal. Later, revelations that some of the arms money Iran paid for the arms had been secretly used to finance the Contra rebels in Nicaragua made the scandal even more damaging. Critics of the administration argued that the secret payments were unconstitutional. They had been made during a time when Congress had forbidden the administration to give any financial support to the Contras. Besides, the critics maintained, the Contras had been using terrorist tactics themselves.

The results of the so-called Iranscam scandal are still being felt as this book is being written. In March 1988, four important figures involved in the arms dealings were indicted for crimes connected to the affair. Among them were the president's national security adviser, Admiral John Poindexter, and a popular Marine Lt. Colonel named Oliver North. North was the first of four to be tried. Jury selection for his trial got underway in February 1989.

U.S. anti-terrorism policies remain in disarray. Even as a means of freeing the hostages, the arms deal with Iran was a failure. Between the time President Reagan authorized the arms shipments to Iran and the time he called them off, only three of the hostages were released. During that same time, four more American hostages were taken. The terrorists actually ended up with *more* hostages after the deal than they had before it was made.

What is more, the revelation that the strongly stated policies laid out in the report of the Vice President's Task Force on Combating Terrorism were being ignored, even while the report was being written, brought all U.S. anti-terrorism policies into question.

The terrorism still goes on.

CHAPTER TWO

REASONS FOR

TERRORISM

THE first step in preparing for any battle is to find out all you can about the enemy you are going to fight. This is as true in the war on terrorism as in any other war. The United States, along with many other countries, has come under attack. It is necessary to ask why. Who are these terrorists? Where do they come from? Perhaps most important of all, why do they do the terrible things they do?

ARE TERRORISTS "CRAZY"?

How can an Irish-Protestant terrorist toss hand grenades among the thousands of mourners at an Irish-Catholic funeral in Belfast, sending deadly shrapnel tearing through the crowd? How can two young Frenchmen set off a bomb on the doorstep of a Paris synagogue hoping to kill whoever happens to be praying inside? How can an Indian Sikh put a bomb on a civilian jetliner without even knowing who will be on board when it blows up? How can Lebanese men and women willingly blow themselves up by driving truckloads of bombs into crowds of people they don't even know?

Most of us cannot imagine doing such things ourselves, and we cannot understand how other people can do them either. Because of this, people tend to identify terrorists with the crazed individuals who suddenly go berserk and attack their neighbors for no reason or who start shooting at people from tall buildings.

It is somehow comfortable to assume that terrorists' actions are not really understandable at all, that they result from some form of insanity. This belief is supported by many politicians and government officials who often refer to terrorist incidents as the "pointless," "mindless" acts of "heartless barbarians."

It is certainly true that crazed individuals and terrorists sometimes commit very similar acts. Both have been known to hijack planes or take hostages or blow up buildings. It is also true that some psychiatrists claim that terrorists tend to be mentally and emotionally disturbed individuals. They explain the terrorists' willingness to commit their awful acts in terms of such mental disorders as paranoia and sadism. Paranoia, they say, causes terrorists to see the world around them as hostile and filled with enemies. Sadism causes them to enjoy the pain of others. Terrorism allows them to strike out at their enemies (real or imagined) and to inflict an enormous amount of pain on other people at the same time.

But many experts on the subject of terrorism argue that it is wrong to dismiss terrorists as mentally unbalanced. Purdue University political scientist Michael Stohl, for example, has argued that terrorists are far from the mindless psychopaths that many people believe them to be. In his book, *The Politics of Terrorism*, he called the idea that "terrorism is the province of madmen" a myth. By that he means that the idea is a widely held but mistaken belief.

Terrorism experts have not denied that many terrorists are mentally unstable. Observation of some terrorists who have been caught has proven that assumption. Many other terrorists, however, seem to be perfectly normal human beings. Some have even become respected national and international figures later in their lives. Few people would argue that Menachem Begin, the Israeli prime minister who won a Nobel Peace Prize in 1978, was "crazy." Yet Begin was the head of a secret group of Jewish guerrillas, known as the Irgun, who fought for the establishment of a Jewish state in Palestine. To drive home their point, in 1946 the Irgun blew up the King David Hotel in Jerusalem killing more than 100 people.

What is more, Begin is only one among many modern leaders who could be fairly accused of having committed terrorist acts. Almost all the revolutions that have resulted in the independence of modern nations have involved terrorist acts. Even the American revolutionaries committed some terrorist acts against British sympathizers in 1776.

In fighting against any enemy, it is important to know where the other side is coming from: what the enemy wants and why the enemy wants it. Some individual terrorists might be "crazy" but not all of them. It is important to understand that terrorists, whether personally disturbed or not, are not acting on a whim. They are acting out of political motives, not psychological ones. If we assume that terrorists are doing what they do only because of personal "hangups," we lose all chance of outwitting or outmaneuvering them.

ARE TERRORISTS CRIMINALS?

If terrorists are not "madmen," then what are they? How can we explain their actions? One popular belief is that they are nothing more nor less than common criminals. That explanation is certainly logical. After all, terrorists commit crimes. Their stocks in trade are assault, bombing, kidnapping, arson, and murder, all of which are against the law in every country on earth. Yet experts have argued that the idea that "terrorism is criminal, not political, activity" is just another myth.

It is not what terrorists do that sets them apart from ordinary criminals, it is their motives. A criminal's motives are intensely personal. They spring from the criminal's individual needs, desires, and emotions. An armed robber holds up a store because he or she wants money to spend, and robbery seems the easiest way to get it. If the robber kills a clerk in the process, it is because the clerk stands in the way of getting the money. If another kind of criminal kills someone, it may be because the killer hates that person for some reason or is so angry that he or she cannot control their own actions. Criminal's motives, then, are always self-centered.

The motives of terrorists, on the other hand, are not self-centered at all. Terrorists do not commit their crimes for private gain or even for personal satisfaction. If asked, many would probably claim that they dislike committing terrorist acts. Ironically, some feel obliged to commit them by their sense of duty. Instead, terrorists' motives are often altruistic. That is, the acts are intended for the benefit of others. Usually, those "others" are a large group of people, a political organization, a racial or ethnic group, or an entire nation. Sometimes, terrorist acts are committed for religious or philosophic causes.

The fact that terrorists can be altruistic was demonstrated by a wave of truck bombings that struck the Middle East in the 1980s. There, the drivers of truckloads of explosives blew themselves up along with their victims. Such terrorists were clearly not acting for themselves but for a cause.

It is important for anyone trying to fight terrorism to understand the terrorists' motives. The difference between their motives and those of criminals means that they will not react in the same ways that ordinary criminals will. Terrorists are not likely to be stopped by the same security measures or punishments that might deter common criminals.

Most criminals, for example, worry a lot about being caught. They fear being injured or killed by the police if they are caught in the act, and they worry about going to jail later. Many terrorists, on the other hand, do not seem to care what happens to them. Like the Middle Eastern truck bombers, some would actually welcome being caught or killed. They would be seen as sacrificing themselves for their cause.

HOW TERRORISTS SEE THEMSELVES

Terrorists do not see themselves as either madmen or criminals. They see themselves as soldiers fighting for a cause. Like soldiers in a war, they deny the charge that they are immoral because innocent people are killed by what they do.

To terrorists, the victims may not be innocent at all. Terrorists sometimes consider all citizens of a country responsible for the actions of that country's government. They refuse to make any distinction between combatants and noncombatants. They do not regard them as individual people, but as symbols: symbols of the nation, government, or policy they represent in the terrorists' mind.

Other terrorists will admit that some of their victims are innocent. It is too bad, they say, but some innocent victims, even women and children, must be sacrificed. This may be a cruel policy, they admit, but no more cruel than the policies of most governments in wartime. They regard the outrage of western governments at the killing of civilians by terrorists to be hypocritical.

They point to the atomic bombs dropped by American planes on the Japanese cities of Hiroshima and Nagasaki in World War II. Those bombs, they argue, were terrorist weapons, designed to inspire terror in civilian populations. They amounted to terrorism on a far bigger scale than anything ever done by any ordinary terrorist. Why, they ask, is it any worse for a terrorist to explode a small bomb on a civilian airplane than for a U.S. airplane to drop much larger bombs on civilian cities?

CAUSES

Ultimately, though, most terrorists justify what they do by the causes they believe in.

People sometimes assume that terrorists regard terrorism as a cause in itself. They assume that terrorists are like members of a single political party, carrying out a single program of violence and fear. But terrorism is not a cause. It is a *means* to an end. It is only a weapon, and like most weapons, it can be used on behalf of any cause—good or bad.

Nothing in this book should be taken to imply that terrorism is good or that terrorists are ever justified in what they do. Terrorism is one of the worst evils in the world today. It is important to understand, however, that bad things can sometimes be done with good motives. That is sometimes the case with terrorism.

In discussing the causes that terrorists believe in, it is vitally *important to keep in mind the distinction between the cause and the terrorist tactics employed on behalf of the cause.* There is no such thing as a terrorist cause. There is only a cause that terrorists espouse.

Every cause supported by terrorists has many other supporters who would never think of taking part in terrorist activity. What is more, if terrorism can be used for a given cause, it also can be used against it. It is not unusual, in fact, to find each side in a political struggle using terrorism against the other side.

Terrorists are so wrapped up in whatever it is they are trying to accomplish that they disregard all other concerns, including human decency. This is particularly true of those terrorists who are committed to an idea, whether political or religious. These

These terrorists, wearing hoods to conceal their identity, hijacked a TWA jet in 1985. They were associated with the Shiite branch of Islam and gained public support of Shiite religious leaders in Beirut, Lebanon. AP/Wide World Photos

ideological terrorists are convinced that they know what is best for the world. What is more, they are sure that history (or God) is on their side. They believe that their ideals justify whatever they do—however bloody and terrible it might be—on behalf of their cause.

Political ideologies are usually divided into two main groups, referred to as the political left and the political right. There are terrorists at both ends of this political spectrum and even some in the middle.

Left-wing terrorists, such as the Red Brigades in Italy and the Direct Action group in France, usually base their beliefs on the ideas of Karl Marx. They see themselves as part of a "people's revolution." They want to establish a political system in which wealth would be distributed more evenly and in which most major economic institutions would be owned collectively. That is, major economic institutions would be owned by the government in the name of all the people.

Right-wing terrorists, such as the European Nationalist Fascists and the many Nazi hate groups, usually see themselves as fighting for a strong, stable society. They believe in a strictly ordered social system, controlled by a wealthy and privileged class, and ruled with an iron hand. They are convinced that only this kind of system can provide peace and order in a dangerous world.

A WEAPON OF THE WEAK

Different terrorists, then, use terrorism to promote different causes. But most terrorist groups have at least two things in common: weakness and desperation. It is often said that terrorism is a weapon of the weak. The strong have other weapons, including wealth and political power, police forces, armies, navies, and air forces.

It is also true that some governments use terrorist tactics to enforce their will. Those are usually governments that believe themselves to be weak and unpopular. If not, why would they have to resort to terror? For the most part, however, the terrorist groups we will discuss here are small and relatively powerless. Their members are a minority, even among those who believe in the same cause. They are faced with an enemy who is bigger and stronger than they are (often their own government). Feeling weak and all but helpless, they turn to terrorism because they see it as the only weapon that offers them any hope.

USES OF TERRORISM

Terrorism has many uses. Among the most common are getting public or governmental attention for a cause, provoking governments into responding, and causing chaos in the society at large.

Getting Attention

Most terrorists are people with a problem. It is usually a problem the rest of the world either doesn't know about or would prefer to ignore. Terrorism is a way to bring the problem to the world's attention, just as the Palestinian terrorists did in Munich.

Terrorism is drama—a drama rehearsed in secret but meant to be performed in full view of the world. Ever since Munich, terrorism has become television drama, played out on the world's television screens. The terrorists are both producers and performers, staging events for the cameras. Sometimes, in fact, they even *own* the cameras. Terrorist kidnappers now often videotape statements from their hostages and deliver the tapes to television news organizations.

It is not the terrorists or their causes that draw the attention of the television cameras. It is their dramatic, violent, and always disruptive actions. Television cameras may not always be on hand to televise the events, but they will be there to record the aftermath. Those pictures—the bomb-shattered buildings, the tangled wreckage of the airplane, the bodies in the streets—will have a powerful effect on the viewers who see them later. If they are powerful enough, they can make the terrorists' cause—their problem—impossible for the world to ignore.

Pressuring People and Governments

Knowing that they cannot defeat their enemy militarily, terrorists try to break down the enemy's will. They hope that the government the terrorism is directed toward will eventually find it easier to give them what they want than to continue living with the constant disruption caused by terrorism.

Sometimes the target government is not the terrorists' real enemy at all. Instead, the violence is directed against some third party. In such cases, the terrorists are trying to give the third party a stake in seeing that their problem is solved. At least some of the kidnappings of Americans in Lebanon, for example, were carried out by the families of seventeen terrorists im-

30

prisoned in Kuwait. The kidnappers hope that keeping American hostages will force the U.S. government to pressure the government of Kuwait to release their family members or at least to give them better treatment while in prison.

Terrorists who target third party countries are, in a sense, telling the rest of the world: "As long as we continue to suffer you will suffer, too. When things are better for us, things will be better for you, too. Solve *our* problem and your problem, the problem of terrorism, will stop."

Provocation

Terrorist acts are sometimes designed to provoke a hostile response from a government. The terrorists commit their atrocities expecting that the government will respond so violently that it will demonstrate its own brutality. They hope that the government's excessive reaction will rally the nation's—or the world's—opinion against the target government.

Governments that misunderstand the motives of terrorists often fall into this trap. Even a relatively small action by a few terrorists can sometimes trigger an enormous response from a government. The kidnapping of just two officials by French-Canadian separatists in 1970 provoked Canada's Prime Minister Pierre Trudeau into invoking the country's War Powers Act to combat the "insurrectionists." Under this drastic measure, the civil rights of all Canadians were technically suspended. Several hundred totally innocent French-Canadians, including many political leaders and the editor of a major newspaper, were at least briefly arrested and thrown into jail.

More extreme terrorist actions can produce much more drastic measures. In the early 1970s, the government of Uruguay reacted to a wave of armed attacks, bombings, kidnappings, and

In 1985, the three television networks featured lead stories on the hijacking of the TWA jet in which Americans were held hostage. From the top are Peter Jennings, ABC; Dan Rather, CBS; and Roger Mudd, NBC. AP/Wide World Photos assassinations by the Tupamaros terrorist group by declaring a "state of internal war." In this case, the object of provoking an extreme response by the government was achieved *too* well. The Uruguayan military ruthlessly crushed the Tupamaros, virtually wiping them out.

Producing Chaos

Revolutionary terrorists hope to produce so much disruption that the government will not be able to function at all. Michael Stohl described the tactic as "the production of chaos...to demonstrate the inability of the regime to govern, to challenge the legitimacy of such regimes to impose order."

Ultimately, these terrorists hope that the government will lose the support of the public. They hope that even people who once depended on the government will lose faith in its ability to govern. Then, when no one is left to defend the government, the revolutionary forces will be able to take over.

CHAPTER THREE

THE GARDEN

OF TERROR

TERRORISM is a worldwide phenomenon. There are terrorist groups in almost every corner of the world. There is one region of the earth, however, where the roots of terror seem to grow deeper and stronger than anywhere else: the Middle East, the troubled region from the western borders of Libya to the eastern borders of Iran, and from the Mediterranean coast of Syria to the tip of the Saudi Arabian peninsula on the Gulf of Aden.

Historically, the Middle East has served as a kind of garden of terrorism. It was there that the seeds of terror first sprouted thousands of years ago, and they are still growing and flourishing there today.

The first acts of terrorism in recorded history took place there, and the first known terrorist organizations came from there. Even today, about 50 percent of all the terrorism in the world originates there. Most of that terrorism has its roots in one or another of three modern countries: Israel, Iran, and Lebanon.

TERROR IN PALESTINE

Like most modern terrorism, the terrorism of the Middle East has its roots in the past. Much of it stems from an age-old struggle over a small strip of land that lies between Saudi Arabia and the Mediterranean Sea. Once known as Palestine and now the site of the modern nation state of Israel, it is also a holy land for three of the world's major religions: Judaism, Christianity, and Islam. Partly because of this and partly because of its location on several important trading routes, it has been a center of conflict for thousands of years.

There was a Hebrew (or Jewish) state in Palestine a thousand years before the birth of Jesus Christ. It had been founded by descendants of the Hebrews who were led there from Egypt by Moses around 1300 B.C. That first Jewish state fell to invaders in 720 B.C. Since then, Palestine has been fought over by a variety of people and empires, including the Jews, the Babylonians, the Romans, the Persians (today's Iranians), the Arabs, and the European-Christian crusaders. By the middle of the nineteenth century, however, the majority of the people living there were Arabs whose families had made their homes in Palestine for many generations.

In Europe, meanwhile, the nineteenth century was a time of extreme anti-Semitism. During this period of hatred for the Jews, thousands of Jews were murdered in waves of organized massacres known as "pogroms." In response, many of the survivors fled eastern Europe for their lives, and many of them set out for Palestine.

Through all the centuries, Jews had continued to think of Palestine as their spiritual homeland. They believed their ancestors had been driven out only temporarily. Someday, they hoped, their descendants would return. From time to time, throughout the nineteenth and early twentieth centuries, groups of Jews had gone to Palestine, forming a Jewish minority who were settled more or less peacefully among the Arabs.

Now, many European Jews began to think, the time had come to reclaim Palestine. It was no longer safe, they believed, to be a Jew in other countries. It was time for them to have a country of their own. Where else, they thought, should that country be, but in their old homeland, the land Jews had been dreaming of for thousands of years?

The Jews who wanted to found a Jewish state in Palestine were known as Zionists. They were met with fear and resentment by some of the Arabs who lived in Palestine, as well as some of the leaders of surrounding Arab countries. Many other Arabs, however, accepted them as neighbors. For a time after World War I, most of the neighboring Arab leaders tried to work out some kind of a settlement with the Jews, but many Palestinian Arabs remained hostile, and occasional mob violence broke out against the Jewish settlers.

In 1922, Britain received a mandate from the League of Nations to administer the situation in Palestine. The mandate included protecting the rights of the Arabs there, while helping the displaced Jews to establish a home for themselves. Britain tried to satisfy each of the groups but ended up angering both of them. It finally announced that it would divide Palestine in two. About one fifth would go for a Jewish homeland and the rest for an Arab state to be known as Trans-Jordan (or Jordan, as it is called today). Both sides felt betrayed by the British. After Hitler came to power in Germany and began persecuting the Jews there, thousands more Zionists fled to Palestine.

Several Jewish groups were formed to pressure Britain into granting them a Jewish state in Palestine. The largest group, called the Haganah, operated as an underground military force. But by 1937, at least one other Jewish group, the Irgun Zvai Leumi (or simply, the Irgun,) had turned to terrorism. Bombs began exploding on Arab buses, in the marketplaces of Arab neighborhoods, and in Arab restaurants: anywhere that Arabs gathered. The terrorism was soon heavy on both sides.

In the 1930s, the Arabs revolted against the British mandate. Their revolt was crushed just as World War II was ready to break out in Europe. For a time during the war, the Arab terrorism in Palestine largely stopped. The Jewish terrorism did not. The Jews in Nazi-occupied Europe were being more ruthlessly persecuted than ever before. Millions were being killed. To the Zionists, the need for a Jewish homeland was more pressing than ever.

A new Jewish group called the Stern Gang, and later the Irgun, continued to attack the British. Britain's anti-Zionist resident minister in Egypt, Lord Moyne, was murdered by the Stern Gang in November 1945.

Once the war was over, the British refused to allow the survivors of the Nazi death camps to come to Palestine. Many of those survivors were refugees, people without a country. Outraged, both the Irgun and the Stern Gang stepped up their activities against the British. An Irgun bomb in the King David Hotel in Jerusalem, home of the British headquarters, killed ninety-one people on July 22, 1946.

THE FOUNDING OF ISRAEL

The British had finally had enough. They appealed to the United Nations to settle the dispute over Palestine. The United Nations announced that it would partition Palestine into a Jewish state and an Arab state. Jerusalem, a city sacred not only to the Jews and the Muslims but to Christians as well, would become an international city. Now the Arabs, who are mostly Muslims, were outraged. Militant groups like the Jihad Moquades (or Holy War Strugglers), a kind of Arab Irgun, stepped up their terrorist activities. Many innocent Jewish civilians were ruthlessly murdered.

But violence came from all sides. In just two months, 46 British citizens were killed, along with 427 Arabs, 381 Jews, and 15 people of other nationalities. The level of violence kept increasing. On April 9, 1948, the Irgun and the Stern Gang cooperated in an assault on the Arab village of Deir Yassin. At first the attackers intended to broadcast a warning, calling on people to leave the village. But the loudspeaker they were going to use was accidentally disabled. The villagers were taken by surprise. In the battle that followed, 200 villagers—most of them women and children—were killed. Reports by survivors, quoted in Larry Collins and Dominique Lapierre's *O Jerusalem!* claimed that many of the attackers had gone wild, killing anyone they found, without regard to age or sex.

On May 14, 1948, the state of Israel was officially born. The next day, armies from Egypt, Lebanon, Jordan, Syria, and Iraq attacked, hoping to destroy the new nation with one quick blow. Instead, the Israelis, well prepared by years of training in the Haganah and the Irgun, drove them out.

BREEDING GROUNDS FOR TERROR

At the time of partition, there were about twice as many Arabs living in Palestine as Jews. Estimates are that there were roughly 1,100,000 Muslim Arabs, 150,000 Christian Arabs, and 620,000 Jews. After partition, Jews poured into Israel while Arabs poured out. Some Arabs were driven away by the new settlers. Others fled because they were frightened of life in a Jewish state. Still others, who had come hoping they would get for themselves some of the land that had been turned over to the Jews, left because their hopes were dashed by the Arab defeat.

Today there are 4.4 million people living within the original borders of the state of Israel. (Israeli territory has been expanded in two wars.) The great majority, about 3.6 million, are Jews.

The partition resulted in more than a million refugees. Hundreds of thousands of Jews fled their homes in now hostile

Arab countries, and were welcomed into the new Jewish state. Most of the Palestinian Arab refugees were not so lucky.

Altogether, about 780,000 Palestinians lost their homes and their homeland in the wake of partition. Some moved reluctantly to the part of Palestine that was now Jordan. Some found new homes for themselves in other countries of the Arab world or in western countries. Among them are many highly skilled and educated people, some of whom have become important leaders in business, politics, and the arts in their adopted countries.

Those Palestinian refugees who were not educated or who had no money were less fortunate. No one wanted them. Whole families had nowhere to go, no country that would welcome them as citizens.

Hundreds of thousands of them were herded into poorly equipped refugee camps in the Arab countries around Israel. They had no choice but to stay there, living in filth and poverty. Like the Jewish refugees before them, they were people without a country. Like those same Jewish refugees before them, they dreamed of one day returning to their ancient homeland of Palestine.

That was in 1948. Many of those same people are still in those camps; so are their children and their children's children. That makes a third generation of exiles, born in refugee camps to parents who were born in the camps themselves.

They have not been able to live in peace, even there. The Israeli government rightly looks upon the camps as hotbeds of resentment against Israel. It knows that Palestinian resistance groups recruit members there. It suspects that much of the terrorism against Israel is planned in the refugee camps. Because of this, Israeli forces often attack the camps, bombing them from the air in retaliation for acts committed against Israel. Following the 1972 attack at the Olympics in Munich, for instance, Israeli planes attacked refugee camps in Syria and Lebanon, killing at least thirty people. Many of those killed were women and children.

Nor are Israelis the Palestinians' only enemies. On the

evening of September 17, 1982, units of an armed force made up of Christian Lebanese moved into two refugee camps in south Beirut, Lebanon. In a brutal attack that went on through most of the night, they murdered several hundred men, women, and children. The killings were in retaliation for the murder of the Christian president of Lebanon by Palestinian terrorists a few days before.

Not surprisingly, the camps have been a breeding ground of hatred and terrorism. Several of the Palestinian terrorists who continue to spread fear and disruption around the world were born in those camps. Among them was at least one of the gunmen who machine-gunned scores of passengers at the Rome airport in December 1985.

PALESTINIAN TERRORISM

Among the many Palestinian resistance groups that sprang up after partition were al-Fatah, the Palestine Liberation Army (or PLA), the Popular Front for the Liberation of Palestine (PFLP), and Al-Saiqa. Each of these groups had its own style, programs, and supporters. Al-Fatah, for example, was what the Palestinians called a *fedayeen*, or commando, organization. The Israelis saw it as terrorist. The PLA, on the other hand, was more like a traditional army. Some of these resistance groups received financial support almost entirely from among the Palestinians themselves. Al-Saiqa, however, was heavily supported by the neighboring Arab nation of Syria.

In May 1964, sixteen years after partition, the major Palestinian groups decided to band together as the Palestine Liberation Organization, or PLO. The different groups would keep their individual identities, but the PLO would coordinate them and speak for them. The PLO's main goal was to destroy Israel and establish a Palestinian state in its place.

In 1967, armies from Egypt, Jordan, and Syria gathered at Israel's border. Without waiting to be attacked itself, Israel attacked them. In the so-called Six Day War that followed, Israel not only defeated the Arab armies massed against it, but conquered much of the territory that had rimmed its borders. It included the areas known as the Golan Heights, the Gaza Strip, and the West Bank of the Jordan River, as well as the entire city of Jerusalem.

Israel has occupied those territories ever since. Some Israelis argue that Israel has a permanent right to them because they were a part of the ancient Jewish homeland. Others say that Israel must only hold them temporarily to protect itself against future attacks from its Arab neighbors. In any case, under military occupation, both the West Bank and Gaza have become new breeding grounds for bitterness, hatred, and, of course, terrorism.

After the defeat of the Arab armies, al-Fatah and its leader, Yasir Arafat, took control of the PLO. From its headquarters in Jordan, the PLO and its members stepped up their terrorist activities against Israel. Bombs were set off in Israeli markets, airports, and even schools. The PLO soon became infamous as the leading practitioner of terrorism in the world, expanding into international terrorism as well, bombing and killing far away from Israel.

It has to be understood that the vast majority of Palestinians are not terrorists. Terrorists are always a minority, and usually a tiny minority, in any society. It is a sign of the anger, frustration, and desperation of the Palestinians today, however, that almost all of them look to the PLO for leadership. In a recent poll conducted by a Palestinian news organization, 93 percent of Palestinians said they believe that the PLO represents them.

In recent years, the PLO has pledged to give up international terrorism. Arafat now condemns any killing of civilians.

The most notorious of the current Palestinian terrorist groups are no longer associated with the PLO. Some are actively opposed to the PLO because they think it wants a negotiated settlement with Israel. The Fatah Revolutionary Council, headed by Abu Nidal, and the Popular Front for the Liberation

Dr. George Habash, leader of the Popular Front for the Liberation of Palestine (PFLP), is shown here, seated second from left, with Palestinians who were deported from the Israeli-held West Bank territory in 1988. AP/Wide World Photos

of Palestine (or PFLP), headed by Dr.George Habash, are the two most important examples. Along with some others, they even launched a terrorist campaign against the PLO itself, murdering PLO leaders and trying to destroy the organization. A direct assault against the PLO headquarters building almost killed Yasir Arafat.

For decades, the Palestinian terrorists have been symbols of terrorism around the world. Their activities may soon pale in comparison with a new brand of terrorism that has sprung up in the Middle East. Already every bit as deadly as Palestinian terrorism ever was, it is perhaps even more dangerous to the

41

peace of the world. It is the Shiite Muslim terrorism centered in Iran and Lebanon.

THE ASSASSINS

Islam, whose followers are called Muslims, is one of the world's most practiced religions. It has many things in common with Judaism and Christianity, including a devotion to one God, whom the Muslims call Allah, and a belief that all human beings are valuable in the eyes of that God. Like the other great religions, however, it has several factions, some of which are fanatical in their beliefs and practices.

The new breed of Middle Eastern terrorists are followers of a fanatical branch of Islam. They can be considered the spiritual heirs of an eleventh-century Middle Eastern society called the Nizaris. Founded by a man known as Sheikh al-Jabal, the Nizaris were members of the Ismaili religious sect. The Ismailis, in turn, were an offshoot of a larger Islamic or Muslim sect known as the Shia, or Shiites.

Al-Jabal ruled the Nizaris from the secret fortress called Alamut, high on a mountaintop in Persia (now Iran). He became notorious throughout Europe as the "Old Man of the Mountain." His followers became equally infamous as the "Hashish-ins," a title given them because the Europeans believed they smoked the drug hashish. "Hashish-in" became simplified as "Assassin," a word that soon became another term for killer because that is what the Assassins were best known for: killing their enemies swiftly and without mercy.

The Shiites were always a minority in the Islamic world. Most Muslims were then, as now, members of the Sunni sect. The Shiites, however, considered the Sunnis heretics. They accused them of betraying the fundamental teachings of the prophet Muhammad, who founded Islam in the seventh century.

In the Muslim world, religion and politics tend to be mixed, and the division between the Shiite and Sunni sects was not only religious but political. The Shia traced their heritage to Ali, the son-in-law of Muhammad, and claimed the right to rule the Islamic world as his followers.

The Ismailis were a minority sect of the Shiites. They were based largely in the Shiite strongholds of Persia and Syria, but they sent their deadly agents all over the Middle East. Convinced that they were serving Allah, the Ismailis spread murder and terror wherever they went.

In modern terms, the Assassins were terrorists. Their killings were performed by brutal and fanatical young men known as Devotees. They were so completely devoted to the society that they eagerly gave up their own lives in suicidal attacks on anyone their religious leaders ordered them to kill. They were sure that God would immediately take them into paradise in return for what they had done. In this way, they were like the Christian crusaders who lived at the same time. Many of the crusaders, too, believed their souls would go straight to heaven if they were killed fighting to regain the Holy Land.

Today, there is a new Shiite society in Lebanon whose members seem every bit as willing to kill, and even eager to die, for the Shiite cause as the fanatical Nizaris Devotees were. It calls itself the Hizbollah, or the Party of God.

THE HIZBOLLAH

On October 23, 1983, two trucks roared through the streets of south Beirut, Lebanon. One smashed through the guardposts outside the headquarters of a U.S. Marine peace-keeping force at the Beirut Airport. As it slammed at full speed into the courtyard of the Marine barracks there, the driver detonated the 2,500 pounds or more of explosives that filled the back of the truck. The explosion obliterated the truck and brought down most of four floors of the airport building that housed the American Marines. Two hundred and twenty Marines, eighteen U.S. Navy men, and three U.S. Army personnel were killed.

U.S. Marines search for victims of the terrorist car bomb attack on their command center in Beirut in 1983. AP/Wide World Photos

Only two minutes later, the second truck slammed into a similar compound housing French peace-keeping forces not far away. Once again, truck and building were engulfed in a massive explosion, and some sixty of the French forces were killed.

Responsibility for the attacks was claimed by people calling themselves members of Islamic Jihad. *Jihad* means "holy war." Terrorists using the same title had also claimed credit for a truck bombing that killed sixty-three people, seventeen of them Americans, at the U.S. Embassy in Beirut the previous April.

Islamic Jihad is a general title used by many terrorists fighting to establish Islamic government in the Middle East. The drivers of the two trucks were almost certainly members of the sect known as the Hizbollah.

The Hizbollah is a product of Shiite history, mixed with recent political events in Lebanon. For centuries, there have been Shiite communities in many countries of the Middle East. One of the largest is in southern Lebanon.

Lebanon is a troubled country. Although the vast majority of the people of Lebanon are Arab, they are divided into three main religious and cultural groups: the Shiite Muslims, the Sunni Muslims, and the Christians. The Shiites are the largest of the three groups in Lebanon. For a long time, however, they were also the weakest.

That ended in the 1970s, when thousands of PLO members were driven out of neighboring Jordan into southern Lebanon. The militant Palestinians of the PLO had a way of trying to take control wherever they went.

The Shiites sympathized with the homeless Palestinians, but they didn't relish becoming the unintended targets of Israeli bombing raids because of them. Even more, they didn't relish the displaced Palestinians displacing *them* in their own homeland.

Showing a strength the Palestinians never suspected they had, the Shiites rose up and drove the PLO northward into the Lebanese capital city of Beirut. In the process, the Shiites became an important military and political force in Lebanon. Some observers believe they are now the most powerful, as well as the largest, military and political force in the country.

It is out of this embittered, but newly powerful group of Lebanese Shiites that the Hizbollah sprung. The most radical of the Shiite groups, it was soon inspired and mobilized by events in the nearby Shiite nation of Iran.

THE SHIITE REVOLUTIONARY COUNCIL

While the Shiites are a minority in several Arab countries, they form a majority in the non-Arab Middle Eastern country of Iran. Even Iran was ruled by a Sunni Muslim shah until 1979, when the last of the shahs was overthrown by a revolution that shook the entire Middle East.

Although the Iranian revolution included many political forces, its most powerful figure was a Shiite religious leader known as the Ayatollah Khomeini. ("Ayatollah" is a title of religious respect.) Before long, the Shiite majority in Iran had control of the new government. It established an Islamic republic, based on the Shiite interpretation of Islam.

In the Shiite world, religious and political leaders are often the same people. Shortly after the Iranian revolution, Shiite religious and political leaders from around the Middle East met in Iran. They formed a secret organization known as the Shiite Revolutionary Council. The council's purpose is to spread the Shiite revolution throughout the Middle East. The council hopes to achieve its purpose by supporting not only the Hizbollah but other terrorist groups who share the council's devotion to Islamic rule. These groups are known in the Islamic world as "fundamentalists." They believe they are upholding the fundamental principles of Islam—principles that should rule the world. They dream of a day when a single fundamentalist Shiite government may rule over the entire world.

The Hizbollah may be the most fanatical of all modern terrorists—and the most angry. They seem to have chosen everyone else in the Middle East as their enemies. They don't just oppose Israel and foreign influence in the Middle East, but most of the Arab governments as well. They oppose everyone and anyone who does not share their extreme, and deeply held, religious beliefs.

The Hizbollah are as ferocious as they are fanatical. Like the ancient Nizaris, the Hizbollah specializes in suicidal assaults. They are best known for truck bombs like those that killed the American and French peace-keeping forces in Beirut in 1983.

OTHER ISLAMIC TERRORISTS

Not all the Muslims hoping for Islamic rule in the Middle East are Shiites. There are many Sunnis who also would like to see the secular (nonreligious) Arab governments replaced by fundamentalist governments more faithful to the principles of Islam.

A few of these Sunni groups also have turned to terror. It was, for example, a Sunni branch of Islamic Jihad that assassinated Egypt's president, Anwar el-Sadat, in October 1981.

At the same time, it must be noted that not all the Islamic fundamentalists are terrorists. Like the Assassins before them, the fundamentalist terrorists are only a small twig of one branch of the Islamic world.

In the shadowy world of Middle Eastern terrorism, it is often hard to distinguish one terrorist group from another. Many groups go by several names. Other groups seem to share the same name. At the present time, more than twenty foreigners, including at least nine Americans, are being held captive by terrorists in Lebanon. Among the groups that have claimed responsibility for kidnapping one or more of them are Islamic Jihad, the Revolutionary Organization of Socialist Muslims, the Lebanese Revolutionary Factions, the Oppressed of the Earth Organization, the Khaybar Brigades, and the Jundallah or Vengence Party.

There are many other terrorist groups that operate out of the Middle East as well. One of the most notorious is the Syrian Socialist National organization. Although based in Syria, its agents have been active around the world. It is this group that is suspected of murdering the president-elect of Lebanon in 1986 and of being responsible for several airplane and street bombings in Europe in recent years. It is this same group that attempted to bring Middle Eastern terrorism to the United States in 1987. Three members of the Syrian Socialst Nationalists were caught after smuggling a bomb across the Canadian-American border into Vermont.

WHY DO ISLAMIC TERRORISTS ATTACK THE WEST?

If their quarrel is with Israel and the secular Arab governments in the Middle East, why do Islamic fundamentalist terrorists

In the name of Allah, the Compassionate, the Merciful

To American Policymakers:

You have become more frank and impertinent in demonstrating
your malicious hostility toward Muslims. You are no longer
satisfied with supporting and participating in the Israeli
Zionist's crimes against Muslims in the Arab world. Now
under the cover of the hypocritical slogan of anti-terrorism,
you are more frequently making recourse to U.S. military
might to initiate aggression against the Muslim Arabs.

We declare with full responsibility that such mischievous
actions will not go unpunished. Retribution will be
unmerciful and everywhere. The Americans will experience
for the first time the righteous anger of the Muslims on
their own territory. We will strike at the most vulnerable
points of American imperialism.

Our threats are not empty words! You have already had the
opportunity of being convinced of this.

We blame you beforehand for any victims among American
civilians. You must be aware that our actions are a response
to your policy of terrorism against the Muslims. We accept
your challenge!

Allah is Great.

                    Islamic Jihad

ASSOCIATED PRESS
33 KASR EL NIL
CAIRO

kidnap so many foreigners? Why does their spiritual leader, the Ayatollah Khomeini, refer to the United States as "the Great Satan"? Why do they hate Americans and other Westerners so much?

Some Americans assume it must be because the Islamic terrorists are communists. Most experts on Middle Eastern terrorism disagree. Some of the Palestinians may be communists, they say, but not the Shiites and the other Islamic fundamentalists, who are hostile not only to American capitalism and European-style Christian-Socialism, but to Soviet-style communism as well. They are Muslims, first and last. This was clearly demonstrated in 1985, when a Sunni fundamentalist group calling itself the Islamic Liberation kidnapped and killed a Soviet diplomat.

It is true, however, that the fundamentalists attack Americans and Western Europeans more often than they attack Eastern Europeans. This seems to have little to do with their victim's political ideology. Instead, it has to do with three other things entirely. The first is the simple fact that there are many more Americans than Soviets in the Middle East. The second is that the United States and other western nations tend to support the fundamentalists' hated enemy—Israel—while the Soviet Union does not. The third, and most important, is the fundamentalists' belief that western social values are polluting the moral purity of the Middle East.

Above all, the fundamentalists want to keep their society pure. To them, that means to be true to Islamic law and tradition. They resent all foreign influence in their countries, and that influence comes mostly from the west, and particularly from the United States.

It was western oil companies that came to extract the oil from the Arab states earlier in this century. They brought western

A letter from "Islamic Jihad," threatening terrorist attacks on American territory, was received by the Cairo office of the Associated Press news organization. AP/Wide World Photos values, along with western money, into the Arab world. Those values and that money transformed the Islamic society of the Middle East in many ways that the fundamentalists dislike.

The Shiites and other fundamentalists are extremely conservative in their ideals of personal and social morality. Unmarried women are to wear veils on their faces and robes down to their feet whenever they go out in public. Unmarried couples must not go out together without a chaperone. No one, male or female, is to drink alcohol.

In many places in the Middle East, those values are no longer honored. In big cities like Cairo and Beirut, many rich Arabs live like Westerners. They dress in European and American fashions. The women no longer wear veils, but put makeup on their faces instead. The women wear short skirts and even form-fitting slacks. Bars, cocktail lounges, and casinos, in which unchaperoned men and women drink and dance together to western rock 'n' roll, are popular. In places like these, some Arab couples have so completely forgotten Islamic morality that they hug and kiss in public. Such behavior is hateful to the fundamentalists, and they blame the West—especially the United States—for bringing it to their countries.

David Jacobsen, an American who was held hostage by Shiites in Beirut for seventeen months, astonished viewers of the *Donahue* television show in 1988 by telling them that his kidnappers were "basically religious men." A second ex-hostage, the Christian missionary, Reverend Ben Weir, explained the kidnappers' motives this way: "My captors saw the United States as the personification of evil; and it was their sacred duty to eliminate that influence from the Middle East in order for society to be what it should be."

CHAPTER FOUR

OTHER ENEMIES

THE seeds of terror may flourish in the soil of the Middle East, but they can grow almost anywhere. There is hardly a country in the world that has been completely free of terrorism in recent decades. India, for example, is plagued by leftist terrorists called Naxalities. Several black nations of southern Africa suffer from the activities of the right-wing Mozambican National Resistance, which is supported by the white government of South Africa. Even Soviet institutions abroad have been attacked by terrorists groups like the Cuban-American Omega-7.

In recent years, however, the bulk of terrorist attacks in the world have been directed at a small minority of countries. According to the public report of the Vice President's Task Force on Combating Terrorism, "Half of the worldwide incidents [of terrorism] in the 1980s were aimed at only 10 countries;

one-third of the total were targeted directly at the United States." This does not mean, however, that most of those attacks took place inside the United States. In fact, amazingly few of them did.

Nineteen eighty-five was probably the peak year for anti-U.S. terrorism in the 1980s. That year, according to a chronology prepared by James P. Wootten of the Congressional Research Service, there were 177 terrorist attacks against American targets. The largest number of them, eighty-six, took place in Latin America. Sixty-one took place in Western Europe, sixteen in the Middle East, eight in Asia, four in Africa, and only two in North America. Apparently using different standards for defining a terrorist attack, the Vice President's Task Force on Combating Terrorism came up with seven terrorist attacks against Americans within the United States that year. Even that is still a very small number compared with the worldwide total.

This was not always the case. During the 1960s, there were scores—and even hundreds— of terrorist incidents inside the United States each year. Most were committed by members of groups such as the Weathermen and the Symbionese Liberation Army. These were left-wing terrorist groups that saw themselves as fighting against an unjust social, political, and economic system. In the 1980s, however, most of the relatively few terrorist attacks that took place inside the United States have been committed by right-wing hate groups, like the Order (an American Nazi-like organization) and the Ku Klux Klan.

Today, the overwhelming majority of attacks against American citizens and institutions takes place abroad, usually in Latin America or Europe.

TERRORISM IN LATIN AMERICA

Latin America is a major center of terrorist activity. Much of it is connected to revolutionary guerrilla groups that are fighting the governments there. Very few countries in the region have stable democratic governments. Most are dictatorships of the right or the left. Many of them carry out terrorist-like acts themselves in order to intimidate any possible political opposition.

Some of the most spectacular of all recent terrorist acts have been committed in Latin America. The largest ransom ever paid for the victim of a terrorist kidnapping, for example, was paid in Argentina. A gang of Montoneros terrorists, supporters of the party of ex-dictator Juan Perón, received $60 million for the release of two brothers named Juan and Jorge Born.

More shockingly, the Colombian group M-19 launched an attack on the Palace of Justice in Bogotá, Colombia, in November 1985 that resulted in the deaths of at least 100 people. The dead included eleven judges, one of whom was the president of Colombia's Supreme Court.

Most terrorism in Latin America is committed by citizens against their own governments. Only a small proportion of the terrorist acts there are directed against foreign targets. According to U.S. government figures, for example, only about 15 percent of the international terrorist incidents reported in 1984 took place in Latin America. That figure is probably typical.

The great majority of international terrorist incidents that *do* take place in the region, however, are aimed at American targets. As we have seen, almost half (48.6 percent) of terrorist attacks on Americans in 1985 took place in Latin America. They included an attack by terrorists who raked the customers sitting at a sidewalk cafe in San Salvador with bullets from automatic weapons. Thirteen people, inlcuding four off-duty U.S. Marines and two American businessmen, were killed.

The reasons Americans are often chosen as targets have to do with the United States' high level of involvement in Latin American affairs. Latin America is, as U.S. politicians like to say, in our backyard. The U.S. government is therefore very concerned with what goes on there. It is particularly worried about communist influence in the region. As a result, it tends to support any existing governments that are not themselves hostile to the United States, giving them economic and even military

The Colombian army retaliated with cannon and machine gun fire against the leftist guerrillas who seized the Palace of Justice in Bogotá in November 1985. AP/Wide World Photos

assistance to help them stay in power. This policy makes the United States a natural target for revolutionary forces attempting to overthrow those governments.

Also, most Latin American countries are poor. What wealth there is tends to be in the hands of a small number of people and businesses. Some of those businesses are local, but often some of the largest are foreign. Many are American.

Because the Latin American people are poor, they will work for very little. Because their labor costs so little, manufacturers there produce goods very cheaply. The goods then can be sold in other countries for large profits. Leftists bitterly resent businesses, and particularly foreign-owned businesses, that do this. They accuse them of exploiting (taking advantage of) Latin American workers to produce profits that are then taken out of Latin America and end up in the pockets of wealthy Americans.

For both economic and political reasons, then, most terrorism directed at Americans in Latin America comes from the left. But not all. Individual Americans not identified with either American government or business interests sometimes come under attack from terrorists on the right. A U.S.-born priest, Reverend Stanley Rother, for example, was gunned down in his rectory in Guatemala on July 28, 1981. The murder was committed by a right-wing death squad, presumably because Rother had been too sympathetic to left-wing rebels opposed to Guatemala's military government. That same year, two Americans working for an international labor union organization were gunned down in the coffee shop of the Sheraton Hotel in San Salvador, El Salvador. The pro-U.S. president of El Salvador, Juan Duarte, blamed the killings on right-wingers who wanted to discourage labor union activity.

EUROTERRORISM

Western Europe is second only to Latin America as a scene of terrorist attacks directed against the United States. Most are committed by one or another of a small group of similar organizations, often described as "red" terrorists. (Red, the color adopted by communist revolutionaries for their flags, has long been associated with radical leftist politics.) There is at least one important red terrorist group in every Western European country.

The leading terrorist group in West Germany has been the Red Army Faction, or Baader-Meinhoff Gang. It was responsible for many bank robberies, armed attacks, and murders in the 1970s. The most infamous was the killing of a wealthy West German industrialist, Hans-Martin Scheleyer, in 1977.

The death of one of the group's two founders and the imprisonment of the other led police to believe that the group already had been destroyed by 1980, but they were wrong. The Red Army Faction has claimed responsibility for a large number of bombings and other terrorist acts since then.

Italy's most important urban terrorist group has long been the Red Brigades. It has carried out scores of attacks against government and business leaders. The best known were the kidnapping and murder of a popular former prime minister of Italy, Aldo Moro, in 1978, and the kidnapping of U.S. Brigadier General James L. Dozier in Verona, three years later. In January 1983, twenty-five members of the Red Brigades were sentenced to life in prison, leading the police to hope that the organization was no longer a serious threat. Several of its members have found refuge in other countries, however, and European and American officials fear that they will become active again at any time.

Founded in the wake of the French student movement that peaked in the late 1960s, the French group Direct Action has claimed responsibility for at least fifty bombings and other attacks over the past two decades. Its most publicized exploit was the murder of the head of the giant French auto company, Renault. Several of its members were brought to trial in France in January 1988.

Spain, Belgium, and Greece have all had active red terrorist groups as well. Sometimes called "Euroterrorists," the reds make little distinction between American and European targets. They see themselves as the vanguard, or advance force, of a revolution that will one day triumph around the world. That revolution is directed against the capitalist economic system, as well as against virtually every existing western political institution. To them, not only the United States but all western

The Red Brigades sent this snapshot of the kidnapped American Brigadier General James L. Dozier to a newspaper in Padua, Italy. AP/Wide World Photos

governments represent that same hated capitalist system. An attack on one is an attack on the other.

The reds are not the only terrorists operating in Europe. On the other extreme of the political spectrum are the blacks, right-wing terrorists who oppose existing political institutions because they are too liberal. The blacks are less well known in the United States because they rarely target Americans. Nonetheless, the terrorism expert Claire Sterling refers to a European "Continent-wide Black Terrorist International," which she describes as "made up of former SS officers, neo-Nazis, Fascists, [and] professional anti-Semites." It was blacks and not reds who were responsible for what she describes as "the worst terrorist assault in Europe since the Second World War." In this assault, a bomb killed 84 people and wounded 200 more at the Bologna train station on August 2, 1980.

Jews are often the favored targets of the blacks. The French group that calls itself the European Nationalist Fascists, for example, launched several anti-Semitic attacks in Paris throughout the 1970s and 1980s. Like many other black terrorists, they specialize in bombing synagogues in which innocent people are praying.

TERRORISM IN NORTHERN IRELAND

The single most deadly terrorist group in Europe is neither red nor black. It is kelly green. It is the Provisional Wing of the Irish Republican Army, or IRA. Like the blacks, the Provos, as they are sometimes called, do not target Americans. Nonetheless, the terrorism in Northern Ireland is of particular interest to the United States for two reasons.

The first is because Irish terrorism is probably the most intense to be found anywhere in the world, with the single possible exception of Lebanon. The second is because so many Americans of Irish descent actively support the Provos and even send them money secretly to help them finance their terrorist activities. The British have complained bitterly about this support, but there seems to be little that the British government or the U.S. government can do about it.

The Provos have one overriding aim: to drive the British out of Northern Ireland. The poor, mostly Catholic nation of Ireland had been under the control of wealthy, Protestant Britain for hundreds of years before it won full independence as the Republic of Ireland in 1949. Even then, its six northernmost counties were split off to become a separate entity called Northern Ireland (or Ulster), which was made a part of Great Britain. This was done largely to accommodate the minority of Protestants who lived in Ireland, most of whom lived in those six counties. In Ulster, the Protestants were actually a majority.

The Catholics in Ulster were now in the position of a minority themselves—and, they felt, an oppressed minority at that. Most of the wealth and power in Northern Ireland was, as it still is, in the hands of Protestants. Ever since the partition, the British have kept soldiers in Northern Ireland to help keep the peace there. Not surprisingly, the presence of these soldiers is bitterly resented by many Catholics.

In the wake of the partition, many Catholics and other anti-British citizens of Northern Ireland flocked to the Irish Republican Army. The IRA has been around for decades. It had fought for, and won, independence for the Republic of Ireland before 1949, and it has continued to press for the independence of Northern Ireland ever since.

Some members of the IRA insisted on using terrorist tactics to carry on the struggle, and in 1969 the group split into two parts. The official IRA rejects terrorism, while the Provisional Wing embraces it. The Provos have been carrying on a campaign of murder and disruption against Britain's presence in Northern Ireland for twenty years. During that time, they have murdered hundreds of people. They have set off bombs in Protestant neighborhoods, ambushed and shot down British soldiers, and even launched mortar attacks on police stations.

They know that they cannot hope to defeat the Protestant majority, much less the British authorities, by military force. Instead, they attempt to turn ordinary life in the Protestant neighborhoods into a daily ordeal of tension and fear and to raise the price Britain has to pay for its presence in Northern Ireland.

The Provos do not limit their activities to the borders of Northern Ireland. They often take their campaign of death and destruction across the Irish Sea and into Britain itself. Provo bombs have exploded in popular London department stores, pubs, and even in the historic Westminster Hall of the British Houses of Parliament.

Many ordinary British men and women have been maimed or killed in these attacks, and even the royal family has suffered from them. On August 30, 1979, a Provo bomb exploded on a yacht belonging to one of the family's most popular members, Earl Louis Mountbatten. A famous World War II hero and the last British Viceroy of India, Mountbatten was killed in the explosion, along with his young grandson and another passenger.

In October 1984 the Provos struck directly at the political head of the British government, Prime Minister Margaret Thatcher. A bomb was set off near her suite in a hotel in Brighton, England. The blast missed the prime minister but killed several other guests in the hotel.

Provo terrorism is not the only kind in Northern Ireland. Catholic terrorism has been met with terrorism from the Protestant side. Protestant-dominated terrorist groups such as the Ulster Defense Association (UDA), the Ulster Volunteer Force (UVF), and the Red Hand Commandos have proven every bit as vicious as the Provos.

Between them, terrorist groups from Ireland often kill hundreds of people in a single year. They have made the little country of Northern Ireland, with a territory of only 5,452 square miles and a population of only 1,537,200 people, the biggest victim of terrorism in all of Europe.

CHAPTER FIVE

ALLIES

IN TERROR

THE separate terrorist groups discussed in earlier chapters do not always act alone. Sometimes they combine forces, presenting an even bigger threat to the countries and institutions they attack. As we have already seen, many terrorist groups have interests in common. All the left-wing Euroterrorist groups, for example, share a common hatred of capitalism. More and more in recent years, terrorist groups have come to recognize these common interests and to act on them.

When the Japanese Red Army slaughtered the Puerto Rican tourists at Lod Airport in 1972, it was still unusual for one group to do that kind of "favor" for another. That is no longer the case. Only a few months later, West German terrorists cooperated with Black September in planning the attack on the Olympic Village in Munich. The years since have seen many more examples of terrorist groups cooperating with each other and even doing each other's dirty work.

In the United States, in fact, right-wing groups such as the Order, the Aryan Nations, and the Ku Klux Klan often share members in common. The contacts made between them has led to shared activities. More and more it seems that various terrorist groups around the world are finding new strength in unity. They are banding together to further their own interests, and in the process they are forming new and even larger networks of terror.

THE EUROPEAN NETWORK

There are several reasons one terrorist might want to do a favor for another. The most obvious is to receive a favor in return. Palestinian terrorists, for example, run training camps for terrorists from Europe. In return, the Europeans give the Palestinians help when they want to carry out activities in Europe. In such cases, the groups involved don't necessarily have any other interests in common at all. Their cooperation is merely a deadly form of "you scratch my back and I'll scratch yours."

In some cases, a common philosophy seems to be enough to get terrorist groups to help each other. In other cases, a common enemy is enough. This seems to be the case in Western Europe, for example, where several left-wing terrorist groups have announced an alliance of their own to combat their governments' NATO alliance. Their first effort to unite took place in 1981, when representatives of several European groups met in Paris, France. There were few signs that the alliance had gone into effect, however, until the summer of 1984.

After 1984, according to the former head of the CIA, William Casey:

> ...at least three of these groups, the West German Red Army Faction, the French group Direct Action, and the Belgian

Communist Combatant Cells have apparently collaborated in a concerted terrorist offensive against NATO that reached a fever pitch of violence by February 1985. The terrorists carried out a rash of assassinations, and bombing attacks on institutions associated with NATO and the United States, and western interests like the Atlantic Institute, West European Union, and the European Space Agency."

The international connections of many terrorists extend beyond contacts with other terrorist groups. They include connections to foreign governments as well.

STATE TERRORISM

Some governments actually sponsor terrorist-like activities against their own citizens. Several Latin American countries, for example, are terrorized by government-sponsored "death squads." These secret squads, often made up of soldiers, torture and murder opponents of the government. In Argentina during the 1970s and early 1980s, hundreds of leftist opponents of the right-wing government became victims each year. In November 1981 alone, 1,000 bodies of the people said to have "disappeared" were discovered, apparently murdered by army death squads.

This kind of government terror is sometimes called "state terrorism." But Moorehead Kennedy, among others, believes that this term is misleading. Kennedy, a U.S. government official who has been held hostage by terrorists, argues that internal government terror should be called "oppression" or "tyranny," instead of terrorism. In any case, this kind of state terrorism is outside the main subject of this book.

STATES THAT SPONSOR TERROR

Some governments, however, are connected to terrorism in other ways. It is known, for example, that many governments give help to outside terrorist groups. Some train them. Some give them money. Some supply them with weapons. Some offer fleeing terrorists a place to hide.

At first, it may seem odd that *any* government would help terrorists. Terrorists violate the laws of virtually every country on earth. Almost every government publicly condemns them. Yet many governments *do* give real support to certain terrorist groups. Why? They do it because they think the terrorists will be of some use to them.

Sometimes the governments share a common ideology with the terrorists—sometimes a common enemy. Sometimes the terrorists are willing to do favors in return for weapons or other support. Many of the world's governments are willing to put what they see as their national interests ahead of their distaste for terrorism.

Among the many governments suspected of aiding terrorists in recent years are South Africa, China, Algeria, Tanzania, Nicaragua, the Congo, Zaire, Egypt, Iraq, and the Soviet Union. Only six, however, are on the official U.S. list of governments it accuses of supporting international terrorism:

The People's Republic of Yemen

Also known as South Yemen, the small Middle Eastern People's Republic of Yemen on the Gulf of Aden is one of the most radical of all the world's communist-style states. It has been the site of guerilla training camps for foreign revolutionaries ever since its own revolution threw out the British in 1967. Among the foreign terrorists that have been trained there are members of the Popular Front for the Liberation of Palestine, Italy's Red Brigades, a Basque group known as the ETA, and the Irish Provos, along with Shiite terrorists of the Islamic Jihad.

North Korea

The North Korean government is one of several suspected not only of supporting terrorism but of actually committing it. President Reagan accused North Korean forces of attacking

American planes and of having a hand in the murder of four members of the South Korean government in Burma in October 1983. In addition, one of two terrorists who blew up a South Korean passenger jet confessed that she had been ordered to do it by an official of the North Korean government.

Cuba

The American government charges Cuba with a long history of "exporting revolution" by supporting revolutionary movements throughout Latin America. Some of that support, the U.S. government claims, involves training and supplying forces that take part in terrorist activities. Cuba was officially added to the list of state sponsors of terrorism for its support of M-19, the Colombian guerrilla group that staged the assault on the Palace of Justice in Bogotá in November 1985.

Syria

Like South Yemen, Syria is believed to support the Popular Front for the Liberation of Palestine, as well as the Islamic fundamentalist movement led by Iran. Syria's own agents may have had a role in attacks on diplomats from Jordan and other third-world countries. What's more, it is suspected that Syria may be linked to the vicious attacks on passengers at the Rome and Vienna airports in December 1985.

Libya

Unlike most other leaders of governments, Libya's Muammar Qaddafi has publicly declared his support for international terrorists. Using the huge amounts of money that flooded into Libya from oil sales in the 1970s and early 1980s, he bragged of financing terrorist groups from Ireland to the Philippines. Also, Qaddafi's government has sent out "hit squads" to other countries, whose task is to murder anti-Qaddafi Libyans living in exile abroad. These squads, known as the Al Burkan, or the Volcano, are under the direction of the Libyan government's so-called People's Committees.

Libya's president Muammar Qaddafi is shown here in a photograph taken shortly after Libyan encounters with U.S. forces over the Gulf of Siddra in 1986. AP/Wide World Photos

Iran

As we have already seen, much of the Shiite terrorism in the Middle East is encouraged, and perhaps directed, by Iran. Some non-Shiite terror also may be Iranian inspired. According to a front page story in the *Washington Times* in February 1989, the bomb on Pan-Am Flight 103 may have been planted by Palestinian terrorists acting for Iran. Iran, the story claimed, wanted revenge for the mistaken shooting down of an Iranian airliner by a U.S. Navy ship earlier in the year. Whether it was involved in the Pan-Am bombing or not, Iran remains the inspiration for those terrorist groups who dream of bringing fundamentalist Islamic rule to the entire Middle East.

THE SOVIET CONNECTION

The Soviet Union is *not* on the official U.S. list of states that sponsor international terrorism. Even so, some people who have studied the issue—including some high officials of the U.S. government—insist that the Soviet Union is behind much of the terrorism in the world today.

In her book, *The Terror Network*, terrorism expert Claire Sterling describes a vast interconnected network of leftist terror groups. Behind that elaborate network, she believes, are the Palestinians. Behind them, like a giant red spider at the center of a web, she sees the Soviet Union.

This view was not widely shared by U.S. government officials until Ronald Reagan took office as president in 1981. Until then, most U.S. officials tended to accept the Soviet Union's denial that it actively supports terrorism of any kind. Officially, the Soviets maintain that even those terrorists who claim to be dedicated communists are nothing but misguided "adventurists."

It isn't that American officials believed that the Soviet Union was incapable of supporting terrorist acts. They had no doubt that the Soviet government could be as brutal as any terrorist. Morality aside, however, it seemed unlikely that the Soviet government would feel comfortable dealing with bands of hot-headed terrorists.

The government of the Soviet Union is a highly centralized institution, particularly when it comes to foreign policy. What is more, it tends to be extremely slow moving and even cautious in foreign policy. It likes to direct and control every detail of its relations with other countries.

It was hard for U.S. officials to imagine bands of wild-eyed terrorists fitting into the careful, well-oiled machine of Soviet foreign policy. Sterling argues that they don't have to fit into it. The Soviets don't need to direct or control the terrorists, she says. "Their value to the Soviet Union has been their capacity to disrupt the west in whatever way they see fit, always stopping short at the outermost borders of the Soviet empire."

Like Sterling, some officials of the Reagan administration saw "inexorably accumulating evidence" that the Soviet Union was, in fact, the spider who was spinning the terrorist web that threatened to ensnare the world.

In January 1981, Regan's secretary of state, Alexander Haig, held a news conference in which he accused the Soviets of "training, funding, and equipping international terrorists." From then on, it became commonplace for American officials to complain about Soviet support of terrorism.

Years later, William Casey talked about what he referred to as the "Soviet connection": "It might seem shadowy to some," Casey declared, "but it seems rather clear to me." Like Haig, he claimed that there were training camps inside the Soviet Union and other Eastern European countries where Palestinians and others were trained for "wars of national liberation," and where they received money, weapons, and information to help them in their struggles. Even Casey, however, admitted that evidence of Soviet support for leftist terrorism inside Europe was "indirect" at best.

Most senior American officials still find the Soviet connection "shadowy," as well as "indirect." So apparently do most high officials of America's allies (and fellow victims of terrorism) in Europe. The journalist John Newhouse "raised the question of links" between the Soviets and the terrorists in interviews with high officials of four Western European governments in 1985. "In each place," he reported in the *New Yorker* magazine, "I was given the same answer: Neither the Soviet Union nor any of its client states supports the terrorists in Western Europe."

The Middle East may be a different matter. There is no question that the Soviets have given training and support to the PLO. There *are* training camps in the Soviet Union and other East European countries where guerrilla forces receive military training. The training received there clearly can be used for terrorism as well as warfare. Training guerrillas who later turn to terrorism, some State Department officials would argue, is not the same as deliberately sponsoring terrorists.

If it was, the United States itself would be open to charges of sponsoring terrorists. It ran camps in Honduras throughout the early 1980s to train Nicaraguan Contra guerrillas to fight the Marxist Sandinista government of Nicaragua. There is a great deal of evidence that some Contra forces have taken part in terrorist acts, including attacks on hospitals and schools.

THE CRIMINAL CONNECTION

Some observers, including Claire Sterling, have suggested that many terrorist groups have ties to organized crime. The Sicily-based Mafia is often mentioned as having ties to both red and black terrorists in Italy, for example.

It is easy to believe that the Mafia might be connected in some way to black terrorism, but a tie with the red terrorists seems much less likely. The Mafia is both politically conservative and strongly anti-communist. Still, Sterling insists that there is such a tie and that the tie is money.

She claimed the Mafia and red terrorists have taken part in several joint robberies and kidnappings for ransom. The profits, according to her, were split fifty-fifty. She did not explain why the Mafia, an extremely experienced group of criminals itself, would need or want the help of left-wing terrorists to carry out robberies and kidnappings. The Mafia has been expert at those kinds of crimes for decades.

In the western hemisphere, the ties between terrorists and criminals seem to center on the Latin American drug traffic. This is, as William Casey has admitted, a "rather murky area." Still, it seems clear that there are ties between a number of terrorist organizations and the infamous Colombian drug smugglers known as the Medellin Cartel. The cartel is named after the Colombian city that is the home of the small group of families who control most of that country's large cocaine trade.

Ordinarily, according to Casey, "neither group...would have much to do with one another." But, Casey points out, terrorists need weapons, and the drug smugglers have the money to buy those weapons. The drug smugglers, on the other hand, need safe shipment points for their drugs. The terrorists, who have political contacts in Cuba and elsewhere in Latin America, are in a position to supply those.

In 1988, an anti-Castro Cuban named Ramon Millian Rodriguez testified before the U.S. Senate Committee on Terrorism and Narcotics. He was in a unique position to tell about links between terrorists and drug smugglers. Before being sentenced to forty-three years in prison for his activities, he served as the chief money handler for the Medellin Cartel. Billions of dollars in drug profits had passed through his hands.

According to Millian's sworn testimony, some of that fortune in drug money went to terrorist groups. The cartel's generosity was not based on ideology. It was willing to finance any group that could be helpful to it, whatever that group's political philosophy. To show just how nonpolitical the drug smugglers were, Millian testified, some of the cartel's money went to the right-wing Nicaraguan Contras, some to left-wing rebels in El Salvador, and some to the left-wing Colombian terrorist group known as the M-19.

THE CHAIN OF TERROR

William Casey described the growing alliances between terrorist groups as a chain of terror that "extends around the globe." From the Middle East to Europe and from Asia to South America, the chain is tightening. Somehow, or other, the United States and the other governments of the western world must find ways to break this chain. If not, the west may be strangled by it.

Fortunately, the terrorists are not the only ones who can band together. In the following chapter we will examine one of the most important weapons the nations of the world have to fight terrorism: the weapon of cooperation.

CHAPTER SIX

WEAPONS AGAINST

TERRORISM

THE four terrorists must have felt relieved, maybe even smug, as they soared through the darkness high over the Mediterranean Sea on October 10, 1985. The terrorists and their companion were the only passengers in the big Egypt Air 737 jetliner. They had just escaped from a very dangerous situation, and they were on their way back to the home base of their faction of the PLO in Tunisia.

It had been only three days since they panicked and hijacked an Italian cruise ship, *Achille Lauro*, on its way from Egypt to Israel. They had never intended to hijack it. They had planned to ride as passengers to Israel, where they intended to launch a deadly assault to pay Israel back for an attack on the PLO headquarters in Tunis a few days earlier. When a crew member found some of their weapons, they had been forced to act. Without thinking things through, they took over the ship.

At first, they ordered it to sail to Syria. When Syria refused to let them dock, they ordered the ship to Egypt. On the way, they killed Leon Klinghoffer, an American passenger, and threw his body into the same waters they were flying over now.

After the *Achille Lauro* arrived in Egypt, the hijackers freed the rest of the passengers in return for safe passage aboard the Egyptian jet to Tunisia. They were being escorted by the leader of their wing of the PLO, Abul Abbas, who had gone to Egypt to negotiate their release. Abbas was not happy with them. The plan to attack Israel had not only failed, Abbas had actually been forced to offer an *apology* for their actions. After all, the PLO had promised not to attack non-Israeli targets.

Still, the terrorists must have been relieved. They had escaped from a dangerous situation. They had survived to fight another day. They had not been successful, but at least they were safe!

But they were not safe. As if by magic, lights suddenly appeared in the blackness outside their windows. The U.S. F-14 fighters that had been shadowing the passenger jet through the darkness had decided to reveal themselves. The terrorists stared out in horror as they felt the big plane begin its descent. It was, they realized, being forced to land, far short of Tunisia, by the smaller, but more deadly, American fighters.

The planes landed at an Italian/NATO air base at Sigonella, Sicily, where Italian authorities arrested the hijackers and held them for trial.

INTERNATIONAL COOPERATION

The capture of the *Achille Lauro* hijackers demonstrated one of the most effective weapons available to combat international terrorism: international cooperation.

Without cooperation between the three nations that had been their victims, the hijackers could not have been caught. Italy, whose ship had been hijacked, the United States, whose citizen

At the end of two days of terror on the cruise ship, *Achille Lauro*, the Palestinian hijackers of the ship were escorted by Egyptian security men on a tugboat to Port Said harbor. AP/Wide World Photos

had been murdered, and Israel, which had been the terrorists' original target, each played a vital role in the dramatic capture. None of them could have carried it off alone.

It was Israel that monitored the Egyptian radio signals that showed which plane the terrorists were on, when it took off, and where it was headed. But Israel was not able to intercept the jet. It had no way to track the plane from its takeoff in Egypt to a location over international waters where the plane could be safely intercepted.

It was the United States that provided the super sophisticated AWACS (E-2) electronic surveillance planes that located the Egypt Air jet even in the dark. Then it was American fighters that forced it down. Neither the United States nor Israel could provide a close airstrip for the plane to land. That was provided by the terrorists' third victim, Italy.

Cooperation is vital in virtually every aspect of the war on terrorism.

INTELLIGENCE

The *Achille Lauro* case dramatically demonstrates the value of sharing intelligence (that is, information) in capturing terrorists. Intelligence also is needed to prevent terrorism in the first place. As William Casey has explained:

> We need to know and understand the various terrorist groups—their style and operating methods, their support structures, and their training camps, which sprout up around the world. This is a task of continuing collection and anaylsis of intelligence in which the civilized nations of the world need to cooperate closely.

Already, as the vice president's task force pointed out, "numerous actual or planned attacks against U.S. or foreign targets have failed or were circumvented through multinational cooperation."

LAW ENFORCEMENT

Law enforcement is another area in which international cooperation is vital. At the moment, each country has its own laws and enforces them in its own way. Even inside each country, individual law enforcement agencies are often jealous of their own prerogatives—their turfs. This makes the agencies reluctant to cooperate with each other, much less with agencies from other countries.

Today terrorist acts are often planned in one country, committed in another, and boasted about in a third. There is no way for any country alone to protect itself from terrorism. It is becoming more and more necessary for law enforcement agencies from different countries to find ways to work together.

The logical place to begin a cooperative effort among countries is with the laws themselves. Nations need to agree on what terrorism is and what punishments they want to mete out for it. A first step would be standardizing the laws that deal with terrorism so that what is illegal in one country would be illegal in all. An equally important, second step would be to standardize agreements dealing with extradition, the legal process by which fugitives are taken from a country in which they have not broken a law to another country in which they have.

As things stand today, each nation has to make a separate treaty with every other nation to provide for extradition between them. Many of those treaties dodge the controversial issue of terrorist crimes altogether. Many countries have no extradition treaties with each other at all. As a result, the worst terrorists can find safety from prosecution simply by escaping to the right country.

As the Irish journalist Edgar O'Ballance has written: If the terrorists could find no sanctuary, and if all countries universally agreed to punish or extradite those seeking refuge, the problem [of terrorism] would subside."

SECURITY

Still another important area of cooperation is the protection of diplomats and other international travelers.

The U.S. State Department has been especially active in recent years, training its own people to protect themselves from terrorist attacks. All Americans stationed overseas are required to take a course in "Coping with Violence Abroad." As a State Department publication published for Foreign Service personnel says: "The Office of Security . . . believes that while there are no guarantees in today's volatile world, there is much that people can do to make themselves less susceptible to terrorist violence and to improve their chances of survival should their efforts fail."

The responsibility for protecting diplomats stationed abroad is shared between the diplomats' own government and the government of the country to which they are assigned. As much as possible, American officials are expected to coordinate their anti-terrorist measures with their hosts. At the same time, the United States tries to protect foreign diplomats stationed in this country.

Diplomats are not the only international travelers threatened by terrorists. When a plane is hijacked, most of the passengers are ordinary citizens, with no connection to any government. The U.S. State Department tries to protect American citizens by issuing warnings against traveling in countries where the danger of terrorism is particularly high.

Perhaps the key element in the protection of travelers from air hijackings is the security of airports. That is a job some governments handle much better than others. Security at some international airports is so poor that the airports are notorious as taking off points for terrorists. Probably the worst of them all in recent years is the airport in Athens, Greece. The airports in Karachi (Pakistan), Rome, Vienna, and even Tel Aviv (Israel) have been vulnerable as well.

More international cooperation could ensure that airports in all countries were equipped with up-to-date weapon-detection devices, that luggage and cargoes were more carefully inspected, that passengers were more carefully screened, and that planes were better protected in flight.

ECONOMIC SANCTIONS AGAINST STATES THAT SPONSOR TERRORISM

Economic sanctions can be a powerful way for a nation to express its anger at the actions of another nation. Widespread economic sanctions, imposed by most, or all, other nations could be a very powerful weapon to force a change in a nation's behavior.

When the Soviet Union invaded Afghanistan in 1979, for example, President Jimmy Carter imposed economic sanctions against the Soviets, including a ban on the sale of American wheat to the Soviet Union. The ban was a strong gesture, but it was only symbolic. It could not stop the Soviets from getting wheat, because they were able to buy all they needed from other countries. If *all* the wheat, growing nations of the world had joined the ban, however, it would have caused severe shortages and exerted real pressure on the Soviets to remove their troops from Afghanistan.

Similar bans on sales of needed items to terrorist-supporting nations might cause them to change their policies as well. International bans on the sales of weapons, ammunition, and other needed supplies to terrorists and their sponsors would be especially useful. At the same time, boycotts could be placed on all goods from countries that support terrorism, closing down the markets for their goods abroad.

Steps like these cannot be taken without some sacrifice. The ban on wheat sales to the Soviets, for instance, seriously hurt American wheat farmers who could not find a new market for their grain. Bans of weapons sales would hurt American weapons manufacturers, and boycotts of foreign goods would hurt American consumers. Former U.S. Secretary of State George Shultz and others believe that although "some sacrifices will be necessary...in the long run...it will have been a small price to pay."

The problem so far has been that not enough countries have been willing to pay that price to make strong economic sanctions a real threat. Even the United States, which claims to favor economic sanctions as a weapon, has been reluctant to stick to them. The ban on wheat sales to the Soviets was very unpopular with American farmers, and as soon as Ronald Reagan replaced Jimmy Carter as president, the ban was lifted.

DIPLOMATIC SANCTIONS

Diplomatic sanctions also can be strong expressions of one government's disapproval of another. There are many steps that the governments of the world can take to apply diplomatic pressure on governments that support terrorism.

Governments can refuse to back positions taken by the offending government in international bodies. High officials of government can refuse to meet with officials from the offending country. The number, or level, of diplomats assigned to the country can be reduced. The number of that country's diplomats allowed into other countries can be reduced, and their activities can be limited. Some or all of them can be expelled. As a last resort, diplomatic relations between the terrorist-supporting country and other countries can be broken off altogether.

Like economic sanctions, diplomatic sanctions will be more effective if more countries join in them.

RELUCTANCE TO COOPERATE

Although the need for international cooperation is clear, that cooperation is difficult to achieve. Just how hard it can be has been demonstrated over and over again in the United Nations.

The United States first offered a weak resolution condemning terrorism to the General Assembly in 1972. It was made weak on purpose, in order to win the broadest possible international support for it. Even so, in the key vote on the resolution, only thirty-four countries voted for it. More than twice that many (seventy-six) voted against and sixteen abstained. The abstainees included such western nations as Greece, France, and Norway.

It wasn't until 1985 that the United Nations finally passed a resolution flatly condemning terrorism. It was the first time the nations of the United Nations had ever brought themselves to condemn all terrorism outright. Even then, the resolution could be passed only by consensus. This meant that countries weren't required to cast a formal "yes" or "no" vote on the question. If they had been, the resolution probably would not have passed.

When the nations of the world find it hard to join together to condemn terrorism, it is not surprising that they find it even harder to join together to take strong action against it. There are many reasons for their reluctance. One is fear. Nations that are not now targets of terrorists are afraid they will become targets if they anger the terrorists by acting against them. Nations that are already targets fear making things worse.

Another important reason for reluctance is distrust. Even allies sometimes distrust each other where terrorism is concerned. In 1988, the new CIA director William Webster told a congressional committee that this agency hesitated to share secrets with some friendly countries because he wasn't sure they would keep it secret. In the same way, Webster admitted, some allies of the United States hesitate to share secrets with it for the same reason.

Still a third reason many nations hesitate to cooperate is their fear of giving up national rights and prerogatives. In general, governments are jealous of their sovereignty—their authority over their own citizens and what takes place inside their own borders. They do not want to surrender any part of that authority to any other nation or to any international body.

INTERNATIONAL AGREEMENTS

Despite these and other problems, many nations do cooperate with each other in specific instances. Intelligence is shared. Warnings of possible terrorist actions are given. Sometimes, as in the capture of the *Achille Lauro* terrorists, joint action is taken.

Some western nations have even made formal agreements on steps to combat terrorism. One of the most sweeping was a secret agreement made by several European countries in 1978. It promised close contact between the nations' policy forces, the sharing of information, and the coordination of anti-terrorism strategies.

Another important European agreement, the European Convention on the Suppression of Terrorism, requires its signers to make sure that all terrorists inside their jurisdiction are prosecuted for their crimes.

The United States has joined in several international agreements and declarations on terrorism. Among them are four separate "declarations of unity" signed at major summit meetings held between the United States, Canada, the United Kingdom, France, West Germany, Italy, and Japan, in 1978, 1980, 1981, and 1984. Of these, the first and fourth were the most important.

The first declaration of unity is known as the Bonn Declaration because it was signed in Bonn, West Germany. Aimed at ending skyjacking, it required its signers to end all airline services between themselves and any country that failed to extradite or prosecute a hijacker. The fourth, or "London Declaration," was broader. It called for more cooperation and coordination between national security services, for stricter regulations to prevent terrorists from using diplomatic immunity to avoid being prosecuted, and for review of all weapons sales to countries that support terrorism.

Ironically, one of the most effective anti-skyjacking agreements the United States ever signed was with Cuba, a nation the United States accuses of supporting terrorism. The late 1960s and early 1970s saw an epidemic of air hijackings in which the skyjackers demanded to be flown to Cuba. The United States became increasingly angry about Cuba's willingness to accept the skyjackers. At the same time, Cuba became increasingly embarrassed. In 1972, the two countries reached an agreement in which Cuba promised to refuse to accept future skyjackers. Cuba kept its promise, and the skyjackings to Cuba soon stopped.

Agreements like these may be promising. They are certainly better than no agreements at all. They are, however, still exceptions. They fall far short of building the truly united front against terrorism that is needed if the war on terrorism is ever going to be won.

CHAPTER SEVEN

FIGHTING FIRE

WITH FIRE—

MILITARY RESPONSES

TO TERRORISM

SOME people believe that the war against terrorism is best fought like any ordinary war: with military force. Others disagree, arguing that military force is ineffective against the methods and tactics of the terrorists.

A CASE STUDY IN RETALIATION

Eighteen American F-111 bombers took off from England's Lakenheath Air Base late in the afternoon of April 14, 1986. The planes would be in the air for several hours before reaching their targets early the next morning. Before they did, several Navy A-6 and A-7 bombers would take off from aircraft carriers in the Mediterranean to join them in an attack on other targets in the same country. That country was Libya, a nation the American government was convinced was one of the world's leading sponsors of terrorism.

The attacks came around 2 o'clock in the morning. The Navy bombers struck Libyan air bases near Benghazi, while the F-111s struck at Tripoli, the capital city of Libya. One of their main targets was the home and headquarters of Libya's leader Colonel Muammar Qaddafi, a man former President Reagan called "the mad dog of the Middle East." By daybreak, the attack was over, and the American planes were headed back to their bases.

In the United States, Reagan proclaimed the attack a success. "Today we did what we had to do," he said. "We Americans are slow to anger... [But] I warned that there should not be a place on Earth where terrorists can rest and train and practice their deadly skills. I meant it. I said that we should act with others, if possible, and alone, if necessary, to ensure that terrorists have no sanctuary anywhere."

The air raids against Libya were an example of military retaliation against terrorism. Retaliation against terrorism has been the official policy of the U.S. government since President Ronald Reagan signed National Security Directive 138 on April 3, 1984. The Libyan raids were carried out to punish Libya for its long support of international terrorism and to deter it from continuing that support in the future.

In the immediate wake of the attacks, most Americans were thrilled. For years, they'd been angered by the growing level of terrorist attacks against American targets and frustrated by their own government's failure to do anything about them. Libya, like Iran, had long been blamed for anti-U.S. terrorism. Now, at long last, the United States had struck back. The majority of Americans were not only pleased with what had been done, but they wanted more of it. They hoped that their country had entered into a new phase of the war on terrorism, one in which military retaliation would become the automatic response to any and all terrorist attacks.

The raids on Libya turned out to be the exception, however, not the rule. They would stand virtually alone as an example of

American military retaliation against terrorism for years to come. Many ordinary Americans find this puzzling. They believe that the United States should strike back with all its military might against all terrorists who dare to attack American interests. But anti-terrorism experts and government officials are divided over the value of retaliation as a weapon in the war on terrorism.

ADVANTAGES AND DISADVANTAGES OF RETALIATION

There is no question that retaliation has some advantages. For one thing, it is fairly easy to justify in the eyes of the world. Provided it is kept in proportion to the terrorism it is designed to punish, it is generally regarded as a legitimate form of self-defense.

What is more, there is something emotionally satisfying about the very idea of retaliation. It seems to be tied into a basic human response, the same response that is triggered when someone is hit in the face. The instinct is to hit back: to fight fire with fire, demand an eye for an eye and a tooth for a tooth. Retaliation promises to satisfy three very deep human impulses: the desire for self-defense, for revenge, and for justice, all at the same time.

Retaliation has at least one more important psychological benefit. It counteracts one of the most damaging of terrorism's effects, its ability to demoralize its victims. Terrorism makes people feel vulnerable, frustrated, and, most of all, helpless. Striking back helps to relieve those feelings. It robs the terrorists of the psychological effect they hoped to produce.

Officials who favor retaliation argue that it does something even more important. They argue that it deters future terrorism as well. As former U.S. Secretary of State George Shultz has argued: "Experience has taught us...that one of the best deterrents to terrorism is the certainty that swift and sure measures will be taken against those who engage in it." Officials who believe in retaliation believe that terrorists are like most schoolyard bullies. They are cowards at heart. They find it easy to hurt others, but they are afraid of getting hurt themselves. Once terrorists learn that their own headquarters, neighborhoods, and training camps will be attacked, they will hesitate before continuing their campaigns of terror.

Other experts on terrorism are not so sure. They argue that large-scale military retaliation doesn't necessarily deter terrorism. It may even encourage it. That is because retaliation is, counterterrorist Gayle Rivers said, "merely an invitation for [the terrorist] to think up some bigger or better response."

For one thing, military attacks tend to kill innocent as well as guilty people. The raids on Libya, for example, had many innocent victims, including Qaddafi's fifteen-month-old-baby daughter. The deaths of innocent people, some experts argue, will only breed greater hatred, produce new martyrs, and generate more recruits for the terrorists' cause.

Pro-retaliation experts, however, point to the attack on Libya as a perfect example of the deterrent effect of retaliation. Since those raids, they say, American intelligence has reported a virtual end to Libyan sponsorship of terrorism around the world. But the anti-retaliation experts are not convinced.

If Libya was deterred by the attack, they say, that effect was far from immediate. The anti-retaliation experts point out that even the State Department reported an increase, not a decrease, in Libyan terrorism in the days immediately following the raids. An American employee of the U.S. Embassy is Khartoum, Sudan, was shot and wounded on the very day the raids took place. Two days later, three hostages who were being held by terrorists in Lebanon were murdered in retaliation for the attacks. One of them, Peter Kilburn, was an American. The others were British citizens, killed to punish Britain for allowing the American planes to take off from British territory. The day after that, four Libyans were arrested attempting to bomb a U.S. Officers' Club in Turkey.

Libyan sponsorship of terrorism *may* have dropped off after that, anti-retaliation experts admit, but how can anyone be sure? Much Libyan sponsorship was secret in the first place, at least until Qaddafi began bragging about it. Does the fact that he stopped bragging about it mean that he stopped doing it as well?

Besides, can intelligence be trusted? The raids were ordered because the United States was convinced the Libyans were behind the bombing of the La Belle Club discotheque in West Berlin on April 5, 1986. Several Americans, along with many more West Germans, were killed or injured in the explosion. More than a year later, however, the West Germans arrested a terrorist it claimed had blown up the discotheque. The evidence they uncovered showed that she had not been working with Libya at all, but with *Syria* instead. If so, any retaliation should have been taken against Syria, not Libya. The wrong country had been punished. If the U.S. intelligence was wrong when it said Libya was behind the bombing of the La Belle Club, could it not be just as wrong when it says that Libyan involvement in terrorism has ended?

THE ISRAELI EXAMPLE

Those who favor retaliation often point to Israel as a model of how to deal with terrorists. Israel has the most extreme retaliation policy in the noncommunist world. It retaliates fiercely for every act of terrorism committed against Israeli targets. Israeli policy is so extreme that the former American diplomat Charles Lichenstein has described it as more than merely an eye for an eye. It is, he says, "two eyes for an eye."

In 1953, when a terrorist grenade killed a woman and two children in the village of Tirat Yehuda, an Israeli Army force attacked the Jordanian village of Obiya, killing sixty-nine people. This included many women and children who had taken cover in some of the fifty homes the soldiers destroyed. When the eleven Israeli athletes were murdered in Munich, the Israeli

Air Force attacked refugee camps in Syria and Lebanon and left more than thirty Palestinians dead.

The Israelis have even adopted cold-blooded assassination as a weapon of retaliation. After Munich, Israeli agents were sent to Europe to avenge the deaths of the athletes. On a single day in 1972, Israeli assassination teams murdered a Libyan in Rome (who they believed helped plan the Lod Airport massacre) and a Palestinian in Paris (who they believed had links to Black September). They even have been known to send letter bombs to terrorist leaders in Arab countries.

In general, experts like Lichenstein and Shultz admire the policy of retaliation without publicly endorsing the practice of assassination. They believe that the strength of Israeli retaliation is one of the key elements in Israel's ability to keep from being destroyed by terrorist chaos.

On the other hand, experts who oppose retaliation point out that it has not kept Israel from remaining one of the major targets of terrorism in modern history. Looking at the record, they say, it is hard to see how retaliation has deterred terrorism. In fact, just the opposite seems to be true.

A DEADLY CYCLE

The main problem with retaliation is the fact that it tends to breed retaliation in return. If it is true that every time terrorists have struck Israel, Israel has retaliated, it is also true that every time Israel has retaliated, the terrorists have struck back at her. The following are just two examples:

In June 1975, terrorists attacked a home in Israel, killing two Israeli citizens. In return, Israeli bombers attacked Palestinian targets in Lebanon. Angered by that attack, the PLO launched a rocket attack of its own on an Israeli vacation resort.

A decade later, on October 1, 1985, Israeli planes attacked the headquarters of the PLO in Tunis, Tunisia. The attack was in retaliation against the PLO for repeated acts of terrorism against

In 1985, Israel struck a blow against the Palestine Liberation Organization (PLO) by destroying PLO headquarters that stood on this site near Tunis, Tunisia. AP/Wide World Photos

Israel. Sixty people were killed in the attack, most of them residents of the Tunis neighborhood in which the headquarters was located. Six days later, PLO terrorists hijacked the Italian cruise ship *Achille Lauro* in an effort to launch a retaliatory attack on Israel. The same Israeli attack in Tunis provoked the

Islamic Jihad in Beirut into murdering one of their American hostages, William Buckley.

If retaliation was really a deterrent, critics of the policy argue, terrorism against Israel would have ended decades ago. Instead, it goes on and on. The retaliation goes on and on as well. It is a deadly cycle, the beginning of which is often lost in time. Everyone knows what the last act of retaliation was for, but no one can remember the original act that began the cycle of retaliation in the first place.

It becomes not a matter of an eye for an eye—or even two eyes for an eye—but an endless process of an eye for an eye for an eye for an eye. . . .

OTHER MILITARY OPTIONS

Retaliation is only one way to use military force against terrorism. It also can be used in more conventional ways, each of which has its own advantages and disadvantages as a tactic in the war on terrorism.

"Surgical Strikes"

Air attacks like those against Libya are known as "surgical strikes." They are designed to be as precise as possible, to "take out" very specific targets. They have three major advantages. First, they can be directed against fairly small, carefully selected targets. Second, they can be carried out swiftly. Third, they involve relatively little risk to the attacking forces because few terrorist groups have anti-aircraft equipment.

Surgical strikes have problems, too. The more "surgical" a strike is designed to be, the harder it is to carry out. Extremely accurate and up-to-date intelligence is needed merely to select the targets and to find ways to hit them effectively. One out of every three of the planes sent to attack Libya failed to reach their targets.

What is more, while these strikes carry small risks to the attackers, they carry higher risks to civilians. No air attack can be truly surgical. Bombers do not always hit their intended targets. In the Libyan raids, for example, the bombs aimed at Qaddafi's tent narrowly missed. Other bombs fell in the wrong neighborhood altogether, killing more than 100 completely innocent men, women, and children. Unlike regular armed forces, terrorists do not live in barracks or in military compounds. Often, in fact, they live in crowded cities, among innocent people. Any air attack against them is likely to kill or maim many of these other people, as the Libyan raids demonstrated so tragically.

Commando Raids

Most countries have commando units specially trained for antiterrorist activity. The United States, for example, has 800 commandos stationed at Fort Bragg, North Carolina. Called the Delta Force, it is trained to work in any condition, whether on land, in the air, or even in the water. It is a combined force, made up of members from the Army and Air Force's special operations units, the Navy's Seals teams, Marine reconnaissance units, and a helicopter force from the 101st Air Assault Division. In addition, it receives air support from the 23rd Air Force.

Commando attacks can be much more "surgical" than air strikes ever could be. Bombs cannot recognize their targets, but commandos can. What's more, commandos are able to be flexible. They can adjust to changes in plans or circumstances.

The main disadvantage of commando attacks is the risk involved in putting forces on the ground in other countries. The risk to the commandos themselves tends to be high, and, if a nation's commandos are killed or captured, it can be extremely embarrassing to the government that sent them. Instead of striking a blow against terrorism, a botched commando raid would probably be considered a victory for the terrorists.

These soldiers, members of an army "Special Reaction Team," participate in a simulation exercise, attempting to free a "hostage." AP/ Wide World Photos

Massive Strikes

Large-scale bombing runs or massive bombardments could be used to destroy a terrorist camp or even an entire port, air base, or major industrial center in a country known to support terrorism.

There are two main advantages to this kind of operation. One is that a massive strike makes the most effective use of a strong nation's military power. The other is that it sends the clearest possible message to the terrorists (or governments) involved. That message, however, is delivered at a terrible cost. Massive strikes kill and injure far more people than other military operations.

What is more, a massive military attack on another country is an act of war. A U.S. president who ordered it might well be violating the U.S. Constitution, and most other countries would be likely to consider the attack a violation of international law. Such an attack could make the country that carried it out an outlaw in the eyes of many countries in the world. It could even arouse sympathy for the terrorists.

An example of the dangers involved in this kind of massive strike occurred during the withdrawal of American troops from Lebanon in 1984. The U.S. battleship *New Jersey* stayed offshore from Lebanon long enough to launch a naval bombardment against Lebanese villages in the hills above Beirut. For nine hours, the ship's big guns lobbed one-ton shells into the villages, killing hundreds of the residents. The villages were suspected of harboring terrorists, and the deadly bombardment was apparently in retaliation for the truck bombing of the U.S. Marine barracks in Beirut.

The shelling of the villages was greeted with shock and anger by many people around the world, including some Americans. Even the American diplomat Bruce Laingen, who favors the use of military force against terrorism in some circumstances, described the bombardment as "a stupid mistake [that] poisoned the well against us" in Lebanon.

OTHER PROBLEMS WITH THE USE OF MILITARY FORCE

Along with the specific disadvantages of each of the options discussed above, there are some general disadvantages to any kind of military action.

Certainly no military action ever should be taken lightly. Even William J. Casey, who as head of the CIA argued strongly for the use of military force to combat terrorism, admitted that "the legitimacy of using force against terrorism depends on our willingness to make strong efforts to deal with this threat by means short of force."

What is more, it is important to be sure that any military action is proportional to the terrorism it is designed to combat. It is important to remember that one strategy of terrorists is to provoke governments into overreacting to them. Too massive a strike could be playing into their hands.

In addition, military force has certain important limitations as an anti-terrorism weapon. One is the difficulty of pinpointing a military target. In an ordinary war, this is usually not hard to do. The enemy has clearly defined geographical borders and military forces that wear identifiable uniforms. This is not true in the war against terrorism. As the confusion surrounding the responsibility for the La Belle Club bombing shows, it can be hard to know whether you are even attacking the right enemy, much less for the right reason.

Any time military forces are sent into action abroad there is some danger that the fighting might escalate. A foreign government might react with greater force than was expected. Other countries might join in. Your nation's forces might be pinned down or threatened to such an extent that more troops would have to be sent in to save them. Before long, what was meant to be a limited, even "surgical," action can easily escalate into large-scale warfare.

Military action often has complex and unpredictable political, economic, and diplomatic effects as well. As Bruce Laingen has pointed out, "No one knows that better than presidents who sit in the Oval Office. Mr. Carter knew that. Mr. Reagan came to know it." It is this unpredictability that explains why American presidents have been so reluctant to use massive military force against terrorists.

TERROR AGAINST TERROR

There is still one more way that military force of a particular kind can be used to combat terrorism. That is by turning the weapons of terrorism back against the terrorists themselves—by fighting terror with terror.

The French government tried to do this in the French colony of Algeria in 1961. Facing a terrorist group called the Delta Commandos, the government established a secret terrorist organization of its own called *La Talion* (which means "retaliation"). *La Talion* was ordered to fight the Delta Commandos on their terms. Within a few months, however, the better trained, more able, and more ruthless Delta Commandos managed to kill off many of the members of *La Talion* and to send the rest scurrying out of the country. The failure of *La Talion* does not mean that it is impossible to defeat terror with terror, however. It only means that the French force was not competent enough, or vicious enough, to do the job. The fact that it can be done was proven in 1981 in Colombia, South America.

To the outside world, Colombia is known mostly for four things. Two of them—high-quality coffee beans and even higher quality emeralds—are matters of pride to Colombians. The other two are not. They are the notorious terrorist group M-19 and the equally notorious drug smuggling ring known as the Medellin Cartel. In late 1980, these two groups came into conflict when M-19 made the mistake of kidnapping a female member of one of the families that make up the cartel. In response, the cartel launched its own terrorist war against M-19.

According to the testimony of Ramon Millian Rodriguez before a U.S. Senate committee, the cartel put some 2,000 criminals into the streets and jungles of Colombia to wipe out M-19. They almost succeeded. They could have done it, but at the last moment, the cartel leaders changed their mind. They decided that they could use the remaining terrorists' own criminal expertise and international contacts. So, when the shattered remnants of the once powerful terrorist group pleaded for peace, the cartel allowed them to survive.

But the Medellin Cartel had shown what it takes to defeat terrorists with their own weapons. Millian Rodriguez, who helped to teach the cartel how to defeat them, described his strategy in chilling terms:

> We taught these people how to become terrorists. We taught them how their enemies would react, and how they should react to counter that. . . . Because an urban guerrilla will use a child as a shield. And, if you want to win a war against them, you have to have men behind a gun who will shoot through the child.

In other words, in order to fight terrorists with their own weapons, you have to become even more vicious and merciless than they are. This is not a path that most civilized governments have been willing to take. If they did, they would cease to be civilized. They would become the thing they were fighting and destroy the vital line between themselves and the terrorists.

CHAPTER EIGHT

HOSTAGES

HOSTAGE taking is one of the most common forms of terrorism. It is also one of the most difficult for authorities to deal with. Black September took the Israeli athletes hostage in Munich in 1972, and the result was a disastrous gun battle. Skyjackers take whole planeloads of passengers hostage, often resulting in long dramas ending in tragedy. Muslim fundamentalist terrorists have been holding several Americans and other westerners hostage in Lebanon for several years.

Terrorists take hostages for many reasons. Hostages provide them with certain publicity, as well as with bargaining chips to trade. Also, hostages provide them with a certain degree of protection. As long as they hold hostages, the authorities will be reluctant to take violent action against them. They will not want to risk the hostages being hurt or killed.

A SPECIAL CHALLENGE

Terrorists who take hostages present a special challenge to the authorities that have to deal with them. It is not just that innocent lives are at stake. Innocent lives are *always* at stake when terrorists are involved. It is the fact that the terrorists try to make the authorities, and not themselves, ultimately responsible for those lives.

Hostage takers present authorities with a painful dilemma. "Do what we want," they say, "and the hostages will live. Don't do what we want, and they will die. And if they do, it will be *your* fault, not ours. *You* will have made the decision that killed them, not us. The choice is yours."

It is, of course, an unfair choice. It is the terrorists who put the hostages at risk, and it is the terrorists who are threatening to kill them. Even though the choice the terrorists present is unfair, the dilemma the authorities face is very real. Should they do what the terrorists demand or not? If not, what then?

GIVING IN

According to the University of Cincinnati's Abraham H. Miller, who has made a study of hostage negotiations, governments give in to terrorists' demands in roughly 56 percent of all hostage takings.

If the safety of the hostages were the authorities' only concern, they would give in to the terrorists in 100 percent of the cases. This is because giving in is most likely to ensure the hostages' safety. The safety of particular hostages, however, is never the authorities' only concern. There is always more at stake in a terrorist hostage taking than the fate of the hostages involved.

Giving in to terrorists means cooperating with them and allowing them to benefit from their crime. Many officials believe that to give in would violate their duty to uphold the law. Besides, many officials believe, giving in might save the hostage being held today at the expense of many hostages to come. If the current hostage takers get what they want in return for their hostages, that will only encourage other terrorists to take more hostages in the future.

In some cases, authorities are unable to agree to terrorists' demands even if they want to do so. Terrorists often ask for things that are beyond the power of any government to give. Such demands are often no more than political gestures or posturing. They are not really intended to be taken as serious requests.

For all these reasons, the U.S. government has declared that it will never give in to the demands of terrorists, no matter how many hostages they hold or what they threaten to do to them. The Report of the Vice President's Task Force on Combating Terrorism states this policy clearly: "The U.S. Government will make no concessions to terrorists." Despite the failure of the government to live up to that commitment in the case of the arms sales to Iran, it remains American policy to this day.

DEALING WITH HOSTAGE SITUATIONS

Once the decision to make no concessions has been reached, authorities face a number of other difficult choices in trying to resolve any ongoing hostage situation. The following are among the options they have to consider.

Censoring the Media

Terrorists who take hostages often demand that the press publish a list of their demands and grievances. There is controversy over whether the press should do so. In some countries, there is serious debate over whether the government

These four men—three Americans and one Indian—were kidnapped from Beirut University College in January 1987. In this photo, released by their captors in 1988, they hold a message urging United States action against Israel to support a Palestinian uprising in Israeli-occupied territories, a move that would allegedly help free the hostages. AP/Wide World Photos

should *allow* the press to publish terrorists' demands or even to report on terrorist activities at all.

The argument for imposing censorship on press coverage of terrorism is obvious. Publicity is one of the main reasons terrorists take hostages in the first place. They want to present their cause to the public. If the press is either unwilling or forbidden to report on what they are doing, they will lose one of the main benefits they hoped to get by their actions. Therefore, some authorities believe, censoring the press might result in a drop in the number of hostage situations they have to deal with.

But would it? Some journalists, at least, are inclined to doubt it. Press silence, they argue, would only cause terrorists to commit ever more shocking atrocities. If merely taking the hostages failed to get them publicity, they will kill one of the hostages. If that fails to get them attention, they will kill more, and so on until they find some threat terrible enough to cause the ban on press coverage to be lifted.

Oddly enough, some terrorists would actually welcome press censorship. Carlos Marighella wrote the book that many terrorists regard as their bible, the *Minimanual of the Urban Guerrilla.* In it, Marighella claimed that imposing censorship on the mass media weakens the government and puts it in "a defensive position." Which is, of course, exactly where the terrorists want it to be. "At this point," Marighella wrote, the government "becomes desperate, is involved in greater contradictions and loss of prestige, and loses time and energy in an exhausting effort at control which is subject to being broken at any moment."

In a free society like that of the United States, press silence would have to be voluntary. Both the tradition of the press itself and the First Amendment guarantee of freedom of the press run counter to any attempt by the government to impose censorship on the news media.

Self-censorship, however, is possible. That is, the news media could refuse to cover certain kinds of hostage incidents or at least refuse to publish the terrorists' demands. The media would be likely to do this, however, only if they were convinced that it would save hostages' lives. The press has, in fact, censored itself to save lives by not reporting on what the police planned to do in certain hostage situations. That is a very different matter from refusing to publish terrorists' demands, much less refusing to cover a hostage situation at all.

As we have already seen, it is far from clear that such drastic self-censorship would help save people's lives. It might do just the opposite. Terrorists, after all, do not threaten to harm their hostages if the press *publishes* information about the situation.

Rather, terrorists threaten to harm hostages if the press does *not* publish such information. Because of that, it is unlikely that the press would accomplish anything by agreeing to withhold information. It is also unlikely that the press would be willing to withhold information. This is shown by the fact that it is hard to find a case in which the press has censored itself in this way in a hostage situation.

Also working against press silence is the competitiveness of the news media. Even if one newspaper or television station agreed to keep silent, another would be likely to go ahead and publish or televise the story, if only to grab its competitor's audience.

The Police Model

When a sophisticated police department is faced with an ordinary criminal who has taken a hostage, there are certain procedures it usually follows.

First, the police surround the place in which the hostage is being held so that the criminal cannot escape. The police then do their best to establish communication with the criminal, either face to face or over a telephone. They try to find out as much as they can about the situation. They seek information about the criminal, the hostage, and the circumstances that led up to the incident. They find out what, if any, demands are being made. Then they open negotiations with the criminal.

Professional negotiators, and sometimes even psychologists, are called in to help. If necessary, some concessions are made to the hostage taker but none that would lead to the criminal escaping with the hostage still at risk.

These steps are all designed to contain the danger built into the situation: to protect the hostage and to keep the incident from getting out of hand. Special Weapons and Tactics, or "SWAT," teams are kept in reserve to take violent action if necessary. They are not used unless there is an immediate threat to the hostage.

The police know that time is on their side. Sooner or later, they hope, the criminal will realize that escape is impossible. Then, tiring of the fear and tension of the situation, he or she will simply surrender. Most of the time, that is exactly what eventually happens. Most hostage incidents handled in this way result in the safe release of the hostage and the arrest of the criminal.

Because of this high success rate, it would seem that the police model would be a good one for governments to follow in dealing with terrorists who take hostages. For various reasons, however, that is often impossible.

First, as we've already discussed, terrorists are not ordinary criminals. They tend to be more determined and less concerned with their own personal safety. What is more, terrorist hostage situations are often more complicated than those involving ordinary criminals. When hostages are held in secret locations, as they are today in Beirut, police cannot take the basic steps necessary to contain the terrorists.

Even in cases where the police model *could* be followed, governments are reluctant to do so. Often, their reluctance comes from the fact that they do not want to be seen negotiating with terrorists.

Refusing to Negotiate

Some governments, including those of the United States and Israel, officially refuse to negotiate over hostages. In some cases, they say, they may be willing to *talk* with the terrorists but never to *deal* with them. This firm stand was reaffirmed in 1988 by U.S. State Department spokesperson Charles Redman, when he told reporters that this policy was "written in stone. No concessions!" he insisted. "No deals!"

Concessions and deals, of course, are what negotiations are all about. Both the United States and Israel have violated their strict "no deals" policies, however. The United States, after all, sold weapons to Iran in 1985 to buy the release of hostages held by the Iranian-supported Shiite terrorists in Lebanon. In 1983, Israel made perhaps the most lopsided hostage deal in recent

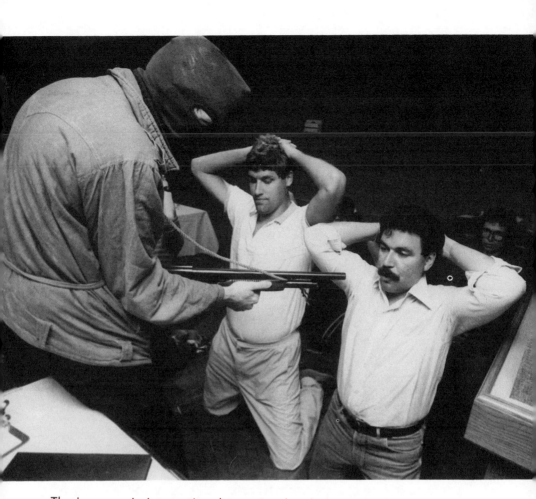

The increase in international terrorism has led some individuals to take unusual security measures. These men are part of a training program designed to teach corporate executives how to handle terrorist attacks. AP/Wide World Photos

times when it released more than 5,000 jailed Palestinians in return for the release of only 6 Israeli prisoners.

Each government could argue that it had not technically violated its official policy. The United States could claim that it had not dealt directly with the Shiite terrorists who were holding the hostages but with the government of Iran. Israel could claim that the Israelis it traded for were not hostages in the usual sense. They were prisoners being held by Arab governments. In reality, both the United States and Israeli governments had negotiated for the release of hostages. Each had made deals with people it knew were actively sponsoring terrorism in return for the release of people being held captive.

Governments are reluctant to negotiate for many of the same reasons they are reluctant to give in to terrorists' demands. The most important is their conviction that negotiations would encourage other terrorists in the future. That belief has been so widely held by U.S. government officials that refusal to negotiate has been the official policy of every American presidential administration since Richard Nixon came into office in 1969.

Nonetheless, many terrorism experts are inclined to disagree with it. Purdue University's Michael Stohl argues that "a simple strategy of non-negotiation, while obviously evidence of firm resolution, does not have any evidence on its side that it will prevent future terrorism." Abraham H. Miller of the University of Cincinnati points out many real life examples that actually point the other way: "Countries in which the government has refused to negotiate—Argentina, Colombia, Israel, Jordan, Turkey, and Uruguay—were nevertheless targets of more hostage episodes."

There are other reasons American government officials are reluctant to negotiate with terrorists. Those reasons could be summed up in the word "appearances." Government leaders worry that negotiation will lend an appearance of legitimacy to the terrorists. It will seem to put them, in some sense, on an equal level with the government with which they are negotiating. At the same time, the government leaders worry that negotiation would make the leaders themselves look weak. It would give the impression that they are being forced to deal with bullies at the point of a gun.

It is interesting to note that this concern about looking weak is more important to government leaders than to the police, who don't seem to worry about it at all. This difference may indicate that government leaders, unlike the police, are mostly concerned about how they will look to the public. In this respect they seem to be less interested in how *effective* their position will be than in how *popular* it will be. Several recent presidential candidates, including Ronald Reagan in 1980 and Governor Michael Dukakis in 1988, have run on a pledge of getting tougher with terrorists. None have run on a pledge that they will be more willing to negotiate with them. This, despite the fact that most law enforcement experts believe that negotiation is a vital tool in dealing with hostage takers of any kind. In general, however, government leaders would prefer to do something more dramatic.

Rescue

It was late in the evening of July 3, 1976 when three Israeli planes swooped down out of the black sky over Entebbe, Uganda. They landed, without lights, on a darkened plain. Within moments, a horde of nearly silent figures had scrambled out of the planes and begun making their way toward the nearby airfield. They were Israeli commandos, and they had come more than two thousand miles to do what they were about to do.

Neither the planes nor the rapidly moving figures were noticed by the people inside the old Entebbe airport terminal. Among them were ten pro-Palestinian terrorists, some of whom were Arabs and some German, along with more than 100 hostages captured when the terrorists had hijacked an Air France jetliner a few days before.

Also near the terminal were several Ugandan government troops who were helping to guard the prisoners. Tension had been high from the beginning of the hostages' ordeal, of course, but it was particularly high that night. The terrorists had threatened to start killing the hostages the next day.

The silence of the night was suddenly shattered by the roar of a nearby explosion. The blast came from somewhere outside the terminal, probably from some distant corner of the airport. Still, it was enough to distract the attention of the Ugandan soldiers long enough for a team of the Israeli commandos to burst into the terminal. Now the silence of the night was shattered by another kind of exploding noise: the deadly chatter of automatic weapons.

Within the next few minutes, thirty people died. They included one Israeli commando, three hostages, seven terrorists, and twenty Ugandan soldiers. When the brief battle was over, 103 hostages and the remaining Israeli commandos were on transport planes headed for safety in Israel.

The Israelis had completed the most dramatic hostage rescue in the history of the war on terrorism. It was daring and heroic, brilliantly planned and expertly executed. It captured the admiration of the world, and it established a model that other governments would love to follow.

Rescuing hostages is much more appealing, to both governments and the public alike, than negotiating for them. It is also much harder and more dangerous. When it works, as it did at Entebbe, it is a triumph. When it fails, it is a disaster. The United States found that out in the spring of 1980.

At that time, some fifty American hostages had been held captive in a secret place in Teheran for several months. They originally had been taken prisoner by a crowd of rioting students, but they were now being held with the coopertion, if not under the direction, of the Iranian government. The Carter administration had found out where they were being held and developed a plan to rescue them.

On April 24, six C-130 Hercules transport planes and 8RH-53 helicopters were sent to Iran. They were supposed to rendezvous in the Iranian desert before heading on to Teheran. Flying over the desert, however, three of the helicopters developed mechanical problems from the sand. When the rendezvous took place, it was decided to scrap the rescue attempt. That would have been bad enough, but as the planes took off, one of the helicopters collided with one of the transport planes and eight men were killed.

The United States was greatly embarrassed when the Iranians gleefully paraded the wreckage of the American planes on the world's television screens. Even worse, the hostages were quickly separated so that no new attempt could be made to rescue them.

The failure of the Iranian mission was far from the worst disaster in the history of rescue attempts. When hijackers killed some of their hostages on board a plane on the ground at Malta on November 24, 1985, Egyptian commandos stormed the plane. The hijackers set off grenades among the passengers, killing fifty-seven people.

The success at Entebbe proves that a rescue mission can be a useful weapon in the war against terrorism. The failures in the Iranian desert and at the Malta airport prove that it also can be a terribly dangerous one. Just how dangerous was shown by a Rand Corporation study of seventy-seven international hostage incidents. Its results revealed a chilling fact. More hostages are killed as a result of efforts to rescue them than are killed outright by the terrorists.

These facts, taken together, suggest that anti-terrorist forces should regard rescue attempts the way most police forces do: only as a last resort.

CHAPTER NINE

THE FUTURE

OF TERRORISM

TERRORISM is a reflection of very real and very deep problems in the world. They range from such ancient problems as the centuries-long split within the Islamic religion to the poverty, hunger, and repression that exist in so many countries around the globe today.

As long as such problems exist, they will continue to breed rage and frustration in the people who suffer from them. Those feelings, in turn, will breed terrorism.

If the problems would somehow disappear, terrorism would disappear along with them. Finding quick and peaceful ways to solve them, then, would be the best possible way to put an end to terrorism. That is not likely to happen soon. In the meantime, terrorism is certain to continue. In fact, it may even get worse.

TERRORIST WEAPONS OF THE FUTURE

The terrorism of the future may be even more terrible than the terrorism of the past. Modern nuclear and chemical weapons have added whole new dimensions to the terrorist threat. Robert H. Kupperman of the U.S. Arms Control and Disarmament Agency describes those dimensions starkly:

A small nuclear bomb could produce a hundred thousand casualties [and] biological agents—both toxins and living organisms—can rival thermonuclear weapons, providing the possibility of producing hundreds of thousands to several millions of casualties in a single incident.

A few years ago, *The Progressive* magazine published an article that explained how to build a small nuclear bomb, one that could fit into a terrorist's suitcase. The writer of the article used only nonclassified, publicly available information to come up with his plans. Building such a bomb would be relatively easy for any skillful terrorist with a scientific education.

Of course, a terrorist would still need enriched uranium to construct an actual working model. Even that might not be too hard for a terrorist to find. The United States has reported substantial amounts of weapons-grade uranium missing in recent years. Some of it was probably stolen and already may be available on the black market.

As Kupperman points out, the right poisons or germs could be just as deadly as a nuclear bomb. A sufficiently deadly bacteria dumped into a big city's water supply, for example, could put millions of people at risk.

DEADLY ALLIANCES

Even without such weapons, the possible future of terrorism is frightening. Consider the possibility raised by Ramon Millian

Rodriguez when he testified before Congress about the ties between the Medellin Cartel and M-19.

A dedicated anti-communist himself, Millian was appalled at the connection between the drug-smuggling cartel and the communist terrorists. In his view, the two groups are natural enemies. The members of the cartel, he says, are "capitalists," by which he meant that they do what they do for profit. The M-19 members, on the other hand, despise the very idea of profit. They do what they do out of devotion to their leftist, violently *anti*-capitalist ideology. What is more, they are as ideologically opposed to drugs as most governments are.

At the moment, however, the two groups are useful to each other, and so they have formed a deadly partnership. For now, according to Millian, the cartel is the dominant partner. He worries, though, about what will happen if that should ever change and M-19 takes control of the cartel.

That would give the terrorist group control of billions of dollars in drug profits. It would enable it to finance terrorism on a scale never seen before. What is more, M-19 would control most of the cocaine coming into the United States. It would be able to increase or decrease that supply at will. That, Millian fears, might give it the ability to recruit, or blackmail, hundreds of thousands of American cocaine users to doing its bidding. Millian pictured a virtual army of drug-addicted M-19 agents, from all classes of American society, willing to commit any atrocities in return for drugs.

BUILDING A WALL OF CONDEMNATION

Nuclear bombs in suitcases, poisoned water supplies, armies of drug-addicted terrorists spreading out around the world. These are truly nightmare visions of the possible future of terrorism.

What can be done to stop these nightmares from coming true? Better security measures, improved intelligence, economic pressures, diplomatic sanctions, negotiations, military rescue operations, each of these may help in certain circumstances. Each can be a valuable weapon in the war on terrorism. None is powerful enough to win it. Something more is needed.

Andrei Sakharov, a Soviet dissident, nuclear physicist, and Nobel Peace Prize winner, has suggested what that something may be. He has called on people around the world to "understand the deadly nature of terrorism whatever its goals," and to deprive *all* terrorists "of any kind of support, even the most passive, and surround them with a wall of condemnation."

What Sakharov understands is that the terrorists, by themselves, have very little power. They are few in number and relatively weak. Their only real power is the influence they can exert on governments, and public opinion, in the world at large. They cannot survive for long without support, whether from private citizens or governments friendly to their aims.

Most, if not all, governments publicly condemn terrorism. Many of the same governments support groups that other nations consider terrorists. Many governments even carry out activities that can be defined as terrorism. As we have already seen, one person's terrorist is another person's freedom fighter. Everyone would like to defeat the terrorists. No one wants to destroy the freedom fighters.

Almost every country in the world is sympathetic to some group, or groups, that practices terrorism. Many third world countries support the PLO, which Israel insists is a terrorist organization. Many of those countries, in turn, insist that Israel also is guilty of terrorism. They point to the Israeli air raids on Palestinian refugee camps and to Israeli assassinations of suspected terrorists. Several Latin American governments sponsor death squads. South Africa accuses its black neighbors of supporting terrorists who oppose its white government, while South Africa's neighbors accuse it of sponsoring the Mozambican National Resistance and other groups that practice terrorism against them.

Western nations, too, have supported or even carried out

terrorist-like activities. In March 1988, British agents shot down three unarmed Irish Provos in Gibralter. On July 10, 1985, French government agents blew up the ship *Rainbow Warrior,* while it lay in harbor at Auckland, New Zealand. The ship belonged to the international environmental group Greenpeace. It was to be used for a peaceful protest of French nuclear tests in the Pacific. One crewman on the ship was killed.

The United States has supported the Nicaraguan Contras, although many observers, including members of Congress like Wisconsin's Dave Obey, have accused Contras groups of terrorist activities. The American government secretly mined harbors in Nicaragua in 1984, endangering the ships and crews of all nations trading with Nicaragua. What is more, the CIA published a "training manual" instructing anti-communist guerrillas in Latin America in such terrorist activities as assassination.

If the United States and other western nations are serious about putting an end to terrorism, this kind of activity must stop. As the British author Gordon Rattray Taylor has warned: "While governments actually finance terrorist groups, or give them training, or allow this to be done, or even promote terroristic acts themselves, and if they give sanctuary to terrorists, the problem cannot be solved."

Governments are not alone in supporting terrorists. If the war on terrorism is going to be successful, the attitudes of ordinary people around the world must change. They have to stop confusing the terrorists with the causes that they support.

Irish Americans, for instance, must abandon the idea that the Provos are romantic heroes. Ordinary Palestinians must stop accepting the killers of Black September and the Popular Front for the Liberation of Palestine as their champions. Left-wing European intellectuals must stop regarding the Red Brigades or M-19 as the vanguard of a people's revolution. Right-wing American intellectuals must stop excusing the terrorism of groups like the Contras on the grounds that they are fighting communists.

Once people have changed their own attitudes, they will have to demand that their governments stop giving support of any kind to the terrorists: that they stop funding them, stop selling them weapons and supplies, and stop defending them in international bodies.

The governments of the world must do what Robert A. Feary, former special assistant to the secretary of state for combating terrorism, wrote that the United States must do. They must refuse to accept the idea that terrorism committed in a "just" cause is "patriotic and heroic." Instead, they must insist "there can be no justification, in any circumstances, for the deliberate killing of innocent individuals."

There will never be general international agreement on which political causes are just and which are unjust. That does not mean that there cannot be general agreement on the need to isolate the terrorists. Unfortunately, that agreement has not been reached yet. The people and governments of the world continue to pick and choose among the terrorists, depending on the causes they support.

As long as they do, terrorism will continue to be a problem for peoples and governments alike. It is a price they must pay for their failure to solve the much deeper problems of misery, poverty, and injustice around the world.

TERRORIST AND ANTI-TERRORIST ORGANIZATIONS

TERRORIST ORGANIZATIONS

LONG as it is, this list is only representative. It is far from complete.

Al Burkan, or the Volcano (Libyan government). An underground organization, representing the Libyan People's Committees, and under the ultimate control of Colonel Muammar Qadaffi. It has been responsible for the murder of several anti-Qadaffi Libyans living abroad.

Armed Forces for National Liberation, or FALN (Puerto Rico, separatist). It has carried out scores of bombings in the United States, mostly in New York City, Washington, D.C., and Chicago. The worst was the bombing of the well-known Fraunces Tavern in New York that killed four people and injured at least ten times that many. Presumably still active.

Armenian Secret Army for the Liberation of Armenia (Armenia, separatist). Dedicated to revenge against Turkey for the slaughter of hundreds of thousands of Armenians during World War I and to freeing that part of ancient Armenia that is now in Turkish hands. Responsible for such actions as the murder of the Turkish ambassadors to Austria and France in 1975 and an armed attack on the airport in Ankara, Turkey, that killed nine people and wounded seventy in August 1982. Still active.

Baader-Meinhof Gang, or Red Army Faction (West Germany, left wing). One of the best-known urban terrorist groups, guilty of many bank robberies, armed attacks, and murders in West Germany and elsewhere. Many of its most notorious acts, including the kidnapping and murder of the industrialist Hans-Martin Scheleyer, took place in the 1970s. Said to have cooperated with Black September in the massacre of the Olympic athletes at Munich in 1972. The death of one of the group's two founders and the imprisonment of the other led police to believe that the group had been destroyed by 1980, but it has since claimed responsibility for many new bombings.

Black September (Palestinian, anti-Israel). Thought to be a faction of the al-Fatah wing of the PLO, Black September took its name from the month in 1970 in which the Palestinian guerrillas were expelled from Jordan. First known for the Olympic Massacre of 1972, it has been active ever since.

Direct Action, or Action Directe (France, left wing). Founded in the wake of the French student movement that peaked in the late 1960s. It has claimed responsibility for some fifty terrorist bombings and other attacks over the past two decades. Some officials believe it also was responsible for the murder of the head of the giant French auto company, Renault. Several of its members went on trial in France in

January 1988. French officials hope that their imprisonment will end the group's effectiveness.

European National Fascists (France, right wing). Responsible for a wave of anti-Semitic attacks in Paris in the 1970s and 1980s.

Fatah Revolutionary Council (Palestinian, anti-Israel). Committed to the complete destruction of the state of Israel. Broke from Arafat's PLO when PLO officially abandoned international terrorism in 1974. Headed by Abu Nidal, said to be one of the most fanatical of all the Palestinian terrorists.

Freedom for the Basque Homeland, or Euzkadia Ti Aaskatasuna, or ETA (Spain, separatist). The most violent of the Basque groups fighting for independence from Spain. It has been guilty of a large number of bombings, bank robberies, and murders over many decades.

Hizbollah, or Party of God (Middle East, Shiite revolutionary). A Shiite Muslim group, based in Lebanon. Said to be linked to a "Shiite Revolutionary Council," it was responsible for the June 14, 1985 hijacking of a TWA flight from Athens, Greece, and the murder of an American Navy diver, Robert Stetham, who happened to be a passenger.

Islamic Jihad, or Holy War (Middle East, Shiite revolutionary). Probably the most active of the Shiite terrorist groups linked to the Shiite Revolutionary Council. Responsible for the two October 25, 1983 truck bombings that killed 241 members of the U.S. peacekeeping forces and 58 members of the French peacekeeping forces in Lebanon and several similar atrocities.

Japanese Army of the Red Star (Japan, left wing). Although its members are Japanese, it seems to operate mostly outside Japan, usually on behalf of the Popular Front for the Liberation of Palestine. It is best known for its May 30, 1972 attack on Lod Airport in Tel Aviv, Israel, that killed twenty-five innocent passengers and wounded some seventy-five more.

Justice Commandos of the Armenian Genocide (Armenia, separatist). Its motives and methods are similar to those of the Armenian Secret Army for the Liberation of Armenia. Responsible for the murder of several Turkish government officials around the world, including at least two in the United States in the 1980s. Still active.

Ku Klux Klan, or KKK (United States, right wing). First formed to terrorize freed slaves and carpetbaggers in the south, the Klan continued to commit lynchings and other attacks against blacks, Jew, and Catholics for many decades into the twentieth century. There are at least fifteen Klan offshoots, with a total membership of 4,500 to 5,500 in the country today. Although most are no longer active in serious terrorist activities, four people were killed taking part in an anti-Klan rally in Greensboro, North Carolina, in 1979. As late as 1985, nine Klan members in the same state were indicted for participating in shootings and illegal cross burnings.

M-19 (Colombia, left wing). Responsible for the kidnapping and murder of the American missionary and linguist Chester Allen Bitterman in Colombia, in January 1981; also the attack on the Palace of Justice in Bogotá, in November 1985, that resulted in the deaths of at least 100 people, including 11 judges. Presumably still active.

Macheteros (Puerto Rico, separatist). Claimed responsibility for blowing up nine U.S. jets, on the ground at Puerto Rico's Munoz Air National Guard Base in January 1981. Current activities unknown.

Montoneros (Argentina, right wing). Supporters of the political movement first led by Argentinian dictator Juan Perón. The Montoneros set a terrorist record, receiving $60 million in ransom for the release of two brothers (Juan and Jorge Born) the group had kidnapped.

Mozambican National Resistance, or MNR (Mozambique, right wing). Opposed to the Marxist government of Mozambique, the MNR has ties to the government of neighboring South Africa. It is said to have killed as many as 900 people in 1987 alone.

Omega-7 (Cuba/United States, right wing). Made up of anti-Castro Cuban exiles, Omega-7 has participated in several assassinations and assassination attempts and in the bombing of targets associated with Cuba, including buildings belonging to American firms that trade with Cuba.

The Order, or Silent Brotherhood (United States, right wing). "Christian Identity" group that considers the government of the United States to be a tool of Zionist world domination. Members have committed at least three murders, including one of a Jewish radio personality named Alan Berg who had mocked the order on the radio. Police believe that most members of the group are currently in jail.

Palestine Liberation Front, or PLF (Palestinian, anti-Israel). A pro-Arafat faction of the PLO headed by Abul Abbas. It is suspected of having been behind the hijacking of the *Achille Lauro* cruise ship in October 1985.

Palestine Liberation Organization, or PLO (Palestinian, anti-Israel). An umbrella organization claiming to represent the majority of the Palestinians. Yasir Arafat has been its main leader and principal public spokesman since 1968. Officially, the PLO announced in 1974 that it would no longer participate in international terrorism—that is, outside of Israel.

People's Revolutionary Army, or ERP (Argentina, left wing). Formed in the late 1960s, the ERP specialized in the kidnapping for ransom of important business officials in Argentina.

People's War (India, left wing). A Naxalite revolutionary group, particularly active in the Indian province of Andra Pradesh. Along with other Naxalite groups, it is said to have been responsible for hundreds of deaths in Andra Pradesh and Bihar provinces in recent years.

The Popular Front for the Liberation of Palestine (Palestinian, anti-Israel). One of the most radical of all the Palestinian terrorist groups. It is unusual in that many of its members are said to come from among the Christian (rather than Muslim) Palestinians. Extremely active in intermational airplane hijackings in the early 1970s. Current activities unknown.

Provos (Northern Ireland, anti-British). The terrorist wing of the Irish Republican Army (IRA), which demands the removal of British influence from Northern Ireland and unification between Northern Ireland and the Republic of Ireland. Since the late 1960s, it has claimed responsibility for the great majority of terrorist acts committed against the British presence in Ireland. Its targets include British soldiers, Irish Protestants, and Irish Catholics opposed to Provo terror. Its most prominent victim was Earl Louis Mountbatten, who died (along with his grandson and another passenger) when his fishing yacht was destroyed by a bomb on August 30, 1979. Still active.

Red Brigades (Italy, left wing). The Brigades carried out a large number of terrorist acts against business and government officials in the 1970s and 1980s. The best known were the kidnapping and murder of former Italian Prime Minister Aldo Moro in 1978 and the kidnapping of U.S. Brigadier General James L. Dozier in Verona, Italy, three years later. In January 1983, twenty-five members of the Red Brigades were sentenced to life in prison, leading the police to hope that the organization is no longer a threat.

Sikhs, Militant (India, separatist). Made up of some radical members of the Sikh religious minority in India, they seek the establishment of an independent Sikh state in the Punjab region. They were responsible for blowing up an Air India jet en route from Toronto, Canada, to Bombay, India, on June 23, 1985, killing 329 people. In addition, Sikh guards murdered Indian Prime Minister Indira Ghandi on October 31, 1984.

Ulster Defense Association, or UDA (Northern Irish, anti-IRA). One of the main Irish-Protestant groups determined to combat the terrorism of the Provisional Wing of the Irish Republican Army with terrorism of their own, the UDA has taken part in the indiscriminate killing of Irish Catholics.

Ulster Volunteer Force, or UVF (Irish, pro-union with Britain). A paramilitary force that grew out of the (Protestant) Orange Lodges in Ireland in the early twentieth century, it has been one of the chief opponents of the Irish Republican Army (IRA) since long before the division of Ireland.

ANTI-TERRORIST ORGANIZATIONS

United States

Central Intelligence Agency. The CIA is the U.S. agency primarily responsible for collecting intelligence on terrorist threats to the United States and its interests abroad.

Delta Force. An 800-person commando force, stationed at Fort Bragg, North Carolina, the Delta Force is specially trained for raids against terrorists holding hostages and other anti-terrorist military actions.

Federal Bureau of Investigation. The FBI is the federal law enforcement agency primarily responsible for anti-terrorist activities within the United States.

Police forces. Most large police departments and many smaller ones have SWAT teams or other units trained for anti-terrorist actions.

Secret Service. The Secret Service is responsible for the safety of certain high-ranking federal officials and their families, as well as heads of state of foreign countries who visit the United States. In this role, the Secret Service has the job of thwarting any possible kidnappings or assassination attempts against any of these officials.

Abroad

Most Western nations have police and intelligence organizations similar to the U.S. institutions described above. In addition, the International Criminal Police Organization, or INTERPOL, acts as a clearinghouse for information on terrorist as well as other criminal activity in member nations around the world.

Several western nations also have anti-terrorist commando forces. Two that have served as partial models for the U.S. Delta Force are the following:

GSG9. One of the newer of the European anti-terrorist commando units, GSG9 is West Germany's version of the older British SAS.

Special Air Service. The SAS was founded during World War II. Besides being the oldest ongoing commando force in the western world, it has the reputation of being one of the best.

BIBLIOGRAPHY

BOOKS

Alexander, Yonah, ed. *International Terrorism: National, Regional, and Global Perspectives*. New York: Praeger Publishers, 1976.

Evans, Alona E., and John F. Murphy. *Legal Aspects of International Terrorism*. Lexington, Mass.: Lexington Books, D. C. Heath and Company, 1978.

Farrell, William Regis. *The U.S. Government Response to Terrorism: In Search of an Effective Strategy*. Boulder, Colo.: Westview Press, 1982.

Kupperman, Robert, and Darrell Trent. *Terrorism*. Stanford, Calif.: Stanford University, Hoover Institution Press, 1979.

Liston, Robert A. *Terrorism*. Nashville: Thomas Nelson, 1977.

Livingston, Marius H. et al., ed. *International Terrorism in the Contemporary World*. Westport, Conn.: Greenwood Press, 1978.

Livingston, Neil C. *The War Against Terrorism*. Lexington, Mass.: Lexington Books, D. C. Heath and Company, 1982.

Miller, Abraham H. *Terrorism and Hostage Negotiations*. Boulder, Colo.: Westview Press, 1980.

Murphy, John F. *Punishing International Terrorists: The Legal Framework for Policy Inititatives*. Totowa, N.J.: Rowman & Allanheld, 1985.

Rivers, Gayle. *The War Against the Terrorists—How to Win It*. Briarcliff Manor, N.Y.: Stein and Day, 1986.

Sterling, Claire. *The Terror Network: The Secret War of International Terrorism*. London: Weidenfeld and Nicolson, 1981.

Stohl, Michael. *The Politics of Terrorism*. New York: Marcel Dekker, 1983.

Waugh, William L., Jr. *International Terrorism*. Salisbury, N.C.: Documentary Publications, 1982.

Wolf, John B. *Fear of Fear*. New York: Plenum Press, 1981.

Government Publications

Browne, Marjorie Ann, and Ellen C. Collier. *Foreign Airport Security: Diplomatic Framework and U.S. Policy*. Washington, D.C.: Congressional Research Service Issue Brief, March 4, 1987.

"Gist" [on the subject of international terrorism]. Washington, D.C.: Department of State, Bureau of Public Affairs, August, 1985.

"International Terrorism: 1985." Hearings before committees of the House of Representatives, 99th Cong. Washington, D.C.: U.S. Government Printing Office, 1985.

Mark, Clyde R. "Lebanon: The Remaining U.S. Hostages." Washington, D.C.: Congressional Research Service Issue Brief, January 15, 1988.

"Patterns of International Terrorism: 1980." Washington, D.C.: National Foreign Assessment Center, June 1981.

"Public Report of the Vice President's Task Force on Combating Terrorism." Washington, D.C.: U.S. Government Printing Office, 1986.

Wooten, James P. "Terrorism: U.S. Policy Options." Washington, D.C.: Congressional Research Service Issue Brief, February 16, 1981.

Wooten, James P. "Terrorist Incidents Involving U.S. Citizens or

Property, 1981-1986: A Chronology." Washington, D.C.: Congressional Research Service Issue Brief, April 7, 1987.

Wooten, James, and Raphael F. Perl. "Anti-terrorism Policy: A Pro-Con Discussion of Retaliation and Deterence Options." Washington, D.C.: Congressional Research Service, Library of Congress, July 10, 1985.

Other

Casey, William J. "International Terrorism: Potent Challenge to American Intelligence." *Vital Speeches of the Day*, September 15, 1985.

"Danger Warnings Posted." *U.S. News & World Report*, April 14, 1986.

"Getting Even." *Newsweek*, Oct. 21, 1985.

"The Hate Movement Today: A Chronicle of Violence and Dissarray." New York: Anti-defamation League of B'nai B'rith, 1988.

"Inside Terror, Inc." *Newsweek*, April 7, 1986.

Newhouse, John. "A Freemasonry of Terrorism." *The New Yorker*, July 8, 1985.

Omang, Joanne. "Terrorism Found Rising, Now Almost Accepted." *Washington Post*, December 3, 1985.

Omang, Joanne. "Summer Lull in Terrorism Mostly an Illusion." *Washington Post*, September 7, 1986.

"The Riskiest Kind of Operation." *Time*, December 9, 1985.

Shipler, David K. "A Shadow War Against Terror." *The New York Times*, November 26, 1985.

"Terror's Target Gallery." *Newsweek*, April 14, 1986.

"Text of State Dept. Report on Abu Nidal Group." *The New York Times*, January 1, 1986.

"12 Months of Terror: The Mideast Connection." *The New York Times*, April 8, 1966.

INDEX

Abbas, Abul, 72
Achille Lauro (ship), 71–74, 79,
    88, 118
Afghanistan, 77
Airlines and airports
    bombings and shootings of, 4,
        8, 12, 13, 14, 61, 66, 87
    hijackings of, 27, 96
    international anti-hijacking
        agreements, 80–81
    rescue mission, 105–106
    security measures at, 76
Al-Fatah (Palestine), 39, 40
Algeria, 94
Al-Jabal, Sheikh, 42
Al-Saiqa (Palestine), 39
Anti-Semitism, 34–35, 57–58,
    116, 118. *See also* Israel
Arab-Israeli conflict. *See* Middle
    East
Arab Revolutionary Cells, 14
Arafat, Yasir, 40, 41
Argentina, 53, 118
Armenia, 12–13, 117
Arms Control and Disarmament
    Agency (U.S.), 109
Arms for hostages, 18–20
Army of the Red Star (Japan), 4,
    8, 61, 116–117
Aryan Nations (U.S.), 62
Assassin, origin of word, 42, 43

Baader-Meinhoff Gang. *See* Red
    Army Faction
Basques. *See* ETA
Begin, Menachem, 23
Belle Club, La (discotheque), 86,
    93
Berg, Alan, 118
Black September (Palestine), 3,
    61, 87, 96, 112, 115. *See also*
    Olympic Village
Black Terrorist International,
    57–58
Bonn Declaration, 80
Born, Juan and Jorge, 53, 118
Brown, John, 10
Buckley, William, 89
Bush, George, 17

Canada, 31
Carter, Jimmy, 16, 77, 93, 106
Casey, William, 62–63, 68, 69,
    70, 74, 92
Central Intelligence Agency
    (U.S.), 12, 17, 18, 62, 79,
    92, 112, 120
CIA. *See* Central Intelligence
    Agency (U.S.)
Collins, Larry, 37
Colombia, 53, 54, 69, 94–95
Commando attacks, 90